stories
that want
to be told

The Judith Neilson Institute champions quality journalism and storytelling in Australia and around the world through grants, practical education programs and events with global leaders that will enlighten, provoke and inspire. The Long Lede Initiative is a collaboration between the Judith Neilson Institute, Penguin Random House and the Copyright Agency and seeks to invest in the future of long-form writing in Australia.

stories that want to be told

The Long Lede Anthology

Featuring:

**Arlie Alizzi, Penny Craswell,
Sam Elkin, Liz Gooch,
Dan Jervis-Bardy, Claire Keenan,
Wing Kuang, Esther Linder
and Hessom Razavi**

VINTAGE BOOKS
Australia

VINTAGE

UK | USA | Canada | Ireland | Australia
India | New Zealand | South Africa | China

Vintage is part of the Penguin Random House group of companies
whose addresses can be found at global.penguinrandomhouse.com.

Penguin
Random House
Australia

First published by Vintage, 2024

Cover design by Luke Causby © Penguin Random House Australia Pty Ltd
Typeset in 12.5/18 pt Adobe Garamond Pro by Post Pre-Press

Printed and bound in Australia by Griffin Press, an accredited
ISO AS/NZS 14001 Environmental Management Systems printer

A catalogue record for this
book is available from the
National Library of Australia

ISBN 978 0 14377 935 3

penguin.com.au

MIX
Paper | Supporting
responsible forestry
FSC® C018684

*We at Penguin Random House Australia acknowledge that Aboriginal and Torres Strait Islander
peoples are the Traditional Custodians and the first storytellers of the lands on which we live
and work. We honour Aboriginal and Torres Strait Islander peoples' continuous connection to
Country, waters, skies and communities. We celebrate Aboriginal and Torres Strait Islander
stories, traditions and living cultures; and we pay our respects to Elders past and present.*

Contents

Introduction

The tectonic shifts that hit journalism over a decade ago continue to shake the industry. Every day, editors and news leaders consider what to preserve and what to leave behind. So far, and for now, well-crafted factual long-form writing is proving it has a future. Media organisations understand that it can attract reader times of ten minutes or more, offering deep insights that foster a better understanding of our world. Long-form journalism also holds enormous commercial value, especially when building brand loyalty. Yet Australian newsrooms lack the bandwidth to foster new talent in this field and cultivate the craft of contemporary long-form.

The Long Lede Initiative, a collaboration between the Judith Neilson Institute (JNI), Penguin Random House and the Copyright Agency, looked to invest in the future of long-form writing in Australia by identifying, developing and promoting the next generation of talented writers. It provided one-on-one coaching with some of the best in the business and a program of masterclasses to help mentees develop their writing practice. This book holds the results of this initiative – pieces from nine talented writers on wide-ranging topics from politics in powerlifting to food distribution chains to the significance of cups, from little known queer histories to refugee policy to sexual consent education and more.

All three organisations recognise the vital importance of supporting Australian writers to develop their skills at various stages of their career and in supporting projects that increase readership of their work.

In 2019, before the world was changed forever with Covid-19, the Copyright Agency's Cultural Fund partnered with the JNI to devise a way of supporting book reviews and critical engagement with new Australian writing with the major media mastheads. This partnership supported the publication of over 300 new reviews of Australian books, and a regular poetry column by one of Australia's award-winning poets, investing in connecting new writing with Australian readers.

The initiative was especially crucial and welcome during the pandemic, providing income-generating opportunities for writers as well as supporting emerging reviewers and critics to hone their craft. When the initiative came to an end, the Copyright Agency started conversations with JNI on how best to continue to support Australian writing. It was decided to focus on new long-form writing, creating important pathways for talented and mid-career writers to further develop their skills through mentoring with some of our finest long-form writers.

Penguin Random House expressed their interest and enthusiasm for a long-form publishing project and helped shape the direction and focus of this mentoring and publishing initiative.

The calibre of new work created through this project and with the generosity and skills of the experienced mentors is nothing short of impressive. With the networks forged and the skills developed through this program we are confident that long-form journalism will continue to attract readers and publishers.

We celebrate the nine writers whose work is included in this anthology and anticipate following their compelling and important stories for many years.

Resistance Training

Introduction by
Paddy Manning

Dr Arlie Alizzi is an Indigenous emerging writer, editor and researcher with a substantial freelance portfolio and a unique personal experience as the first 'out' transgender powerlifter to have competed in an internationally sanctioned event in Australia.

Arlie's compelling proposal for this project walked a fine line between telling his own unique story and reporting objectively on a sport and community – powerlifting – which is its own world, unfamiliar to many people.

Arlie has resisted the temptation to make himself the story here and has provided us a rare window into the powerlifting world – a world of often toxic masculinity and 'little big men', which is bitterly divided over the rights of trans competitors. Arlie reveals his own perspective and interest, almost by way of disclosure, but then concentrates on the characters who make this story, told with an anthropological eye for cultural and behavioural details.

I have no doubt Arlie's ability to identify with some of the key characters interviewed on the record has helped him gain not only access, but also a degree of honesty that would be very difficult for mainstream or sports journalists to obtain.

Arlie's own track record as a powerlifter, his decision to come out as transgender and subsequent experience of ignorance, intolerance and discrimination could be the basis of a fascinating follow-up to this essay.

Highly qualified and self-motivated, Arlie has worked hard to refine the initial, very broad, proposal through successive drafts to this powerful final version, which speaks for itself.

Early on, Arlie had indicated the piece might become an investigation into the commercial side of powerlifting – scrutinising the supplement-makers, brands, gyms and social media influencers who are making money out of the sport. Instead of producing a dry piece of business reporting, Arlie has written a powerful human story that has a hard political edge.

The final draft of Arlie's piece is thought-provoking and affecting, the more so because it is written calmly, with a rigorous detachment that inspires confidence in his observations – until it comes to a crescendo, putting the whole discussion in the context of an increasingly hurtful and even violent 'debate' on trans rights, and concludes with a pointed, passionate statement that cuts to the heart of the issue. Arlie's piece succeeds on its own terms.

Resistance Training

Arlie Alizzi

THERE IS AT LEAST ONE GYM LIKE AVIA PERFORMANCE IN EVERY city in Australia. They are located – geographically as well as aesthetically – far away from the comforts of inner-urban commercial or boutique gym spaces. They do not contain pot plants, run classes, display exposed brick walls or usually have air conditioning, and they don't sit in thoroughfares or street malls. They do not have windows you can stare into at people doing cardio in smooth and seamless outfits. Instead, they live in quiet, light industrial areas on the outskirts of towns and cities, often only accessible by car. Think about the foothills about fifteen minutes' drive to the west of Burleigh Heads on Yugambeh Country. Think about the area just beyond the train tracks in South Geelong on Wadawurrung Country, the renovated wharf areas near Footscray, Wurundjeri Country, or the area behind the 'flannel curtain' in northern Hobart, nipaluna. Physically these gyms are nondescript, made of thick sheets of iceberg concrete, high ceilings and roller doors, and while they are independent and unfranchised, their formula repeats enough that you can walk into one and feel like you are walking into all of them. Sometimes you will even see the same people.

Avia sits in a quiet light industrial area of Coburg North near the drive-in cinema, the place where the Merri Creek reaches up to the Fawkner Cemetery and Sydney Road becomes the Hume. It is May 2021 and I am spending a weekend in a small room above the gym to earn a certification in powerlifting coaching. Many of the other participants don't know much about the sport of power-lifting at all. For the learners who are already in the fitness industry, this course will contribute to the professional development points that personal trainers require each year to keep their accreditation with the peak regulatory body of fitness professionals in Australia. Sprinkled among the group are a few beginner powerlifting coaches like me. They are people with other day jobs or in full-time study, whose belonging to the sport is visible in the bags full of gym gear and snacks they carry, the huge muscles on their legs and hips, novelty socks, and clean black t-shirts bearing the logos of one of two popular local powerlifting gear brands.

The lead educator for this weekend, Robert Wilks, president of Powerlifting Australia (PA), has been a vocal proponent of anti-doping in Australian sport for a long time. In 2017 he had a legal battle with the global peak body for drug-tested powerlifting, the International Powerlifting Federation (IPF), over his claim that they failed to properly regulate the sport's anti-doping processes. This conflict led to Wilks' personal expulsion from the IPF committee and, by extension, the expulsion of the whole Oceania and Australian region from IPF-sanctioned competitions. Wilks was at the time the CEO of the only IPF-affiliated federations for that region.

Wilks talks the class through the specifics of powerlifting competition. For the uninitiated, it is a strength sport consisting of a barbell squat, bench press and deadlift, and it is segregated by gender, age and weight classes. Competitors are ranked by a scoring system using an equation to determine relative strength based on body weight, gender and age. For many years, the common equation used was called the Wilks formula, and it was written by Robert himself. Rather than public funding, powerlifting's revenue is mostly driven by membership, and membership is fairly costly, with most of the money going towards running competitions, maintaining compliance with anti-doping systems, travel to international contests, and other administrative costs. Wilks then provides a lengthy list of health risks that present a concern in athletes who dope in sports, and that famously impacted East German athletes back in the 1970s. These include systemic heart, organ and reproductive issues in men, and additional hormonal problems and masculinisation in women. 'Women,' he says, 'run into big problems when introducing testosterone into their system. I have very bad news for them: their clitoris can enlarge. Facial hair grows, body hair, even balding can occur. Bad, bad, bad.'

Uncomfortable laughter echoes through the classroom. Wilks briefly glances over at me when he says these things. I am the first out transgender person to compete in drug-tested, IPF-sanctioned powerlifting in Australia.

During the practical component of the weekend, Robert commands me to help him demonstrate how to teach a sumo deadlift; I will play the role of the athlete under instruction. While he is instructing me, he tells the class that during competition coaching in one rep max–based strength sports like weightlifting and powerlifting, an athlete goes into a state of high physiological arousal that limits their cognitive capacity. As a coach, it is important to be familiar with these states and how to effectively manage them. The athlete's ability to understand complex instructions is compromised. It is advisable, then, to use short phrases, three words or less; one word is better. 'At a powerlifting meet, you are dealing with a group of extremely strong, highly aroused idiots.' Some athletes even perform best if you hurl the odd insult at them. Though this is not really the done thing now, he mentions it was an industry secret around the time Ron Barassi was the coach of Melbourne Football Club that some athletes would take this type of verbal abuse and go out and play the game of their lives.

I get myself into position for a lift I think I know. Robert barks: 'Eyes up. Chest up. Higher. More. More. More. There. Okay. Go.' I find my body arranging itself in response. I have practised sumo as a secondary lift for two years, but now I feel I am doing a movement I have never done before, and it's like magic.

Later, Wilks teaches us how to correct an athlete's competition standard bench press with the help of one of the small crew of volunteers he has brought with him. I have been admiring this woman. She is in her early twenties, short, with bobbed hair, glasses and a clinically precise competition squat. Earlier I watched her unrack the bar and line it up, her gaze perfectly neutral, with no sign of strain on her face. Now, as she positions herself on the bench, feet reaching towards her shoulders, back arched, ribs projecting into the ceiling and chin tucked – the signature pose of a short powerlifter maximising their leverages to the fullest extent – Wilks positions himself between her spread knees and looks down at her body on the bench. 'This,' he comments to us, 'is the centrefold pose.' There is no laughter. We all look at each other.

I later learn this lifter is an elite-level under-48kg athlete named Dori Qu. She belongs to a group of Chinese international student athletes who train at Wilks' club at the University of Melbourne. These lifters are reserved with us, appearing a little socially awkward but intimidating all the same due to their obvious skill and their privileged attachment to Wilks.

The methods Wilks teaches us to produce powerlifting skill and strength are rigid, constrictive and one-size-fits-all. He heavily rejects the innovations of online coaching and some of its emergent strategies. If any athlete comes to us with knowledge that deviates from his model, he advises us, 'They have spent too much time online.' It is a mistake to view lifters, the 'idiots' we are being coached to handle, as people with self-esteem issues, he adds. 'They are narcissists.'

A few months later, an article published by *The Age* reports that Qu has written a complaint to PA's board that Wilks sexually harassed and assaulted her. He has responded by suing her for defamation, along with another elite athlete he used to coach, Victor Liu, for sharing private text messages about the situation, which Wilks later claimed in court had harmed his reputation.

A story plays out in the media over the next eighteen months. Journalists from *The Age* detail the content of Qu's complaint to PA (which had been shared with Wilks by the majority male board), and his subsequent legal campaign against Qu. They examine Wilks' ties to a number of other businesses, his status as a registered psychologist and the wide-reaching impact the case is having on the sport's culture, leaving readers with more questions than answers.

The case added to growing momentum of public discussion about women's experiences in sports in Australia. It also presented a test case for a reform recently made to defamation law in Victoria related to the idea of 'serious harm' done to reputation. This reform was made in response to a rapid increase in the number of defamation suits in Victoria over the pandemic years, attributed to a rise in legal disputes over things like abusive social media posts and negative reviews, which debatably do not seriously damage a reputation enough to warrant the court's involvement. Wilks' claim that his reputation was harmed by Qu will test this idea in court for the first time. At the time of writing, the matter is still awaiting trial.

When it comes to how we understand and respond to conflict, abuse and harm, there is a disconnect between the way laws are written and interpreted in court and the way the events are experienced and interpreted in communities. While many in the powerlifting world had shown ambivalence towards or measured support for Wilks' campaign against the IPF, there were lingering questions about his legal pursuit of individuals like Sean Muir, a powerlifter who established the Australian Powerlifting Union (APU) as an IPF affiliate (and therefore a rival to Wilks' Powerlifting Australia) in 2018 following the split. Like Qu, Muir was sued by Wilks after sending an email to the PA board in which he expressed what was, to him, reasoned concern about Wilks' conduct towards the IPF and its impact on Australian sport. Muir's new federation survived this legal battle and continues to gain followers in Australia.

*

Australian powerlifting is not regulated, overseen or significantly invested in by the Australian Institute of Sport (AIS), and has not yet gained a place in either the Olympics or the Commonwealth Games outside of the Para-Commonwealth Games.

While not yet fully achieving the international status that some of its participants desire, powerlifting has become an increasingly accessible world over the last two decades. This has meant a rapid diversification. Women's participation has notably increased at both competitive and local levels. At a lower, slower rate, and with a few more concrete barriers to overcome, the participation of trans athletes in Australia has also increased.

As powerlifting has become more mainstream and even more ambitious in its wishes for Olympic inclusion, it has had to grapple with the demands of international sporting bodies in a high-stakes competition for recognition and legitimacy. It must also serve the needs of a new and much more diverse (and sometimes ideologically divergent) population of participants.

It would be easy to cite social media as the main driver for the recent mainstreaming of powerlifting, given the increasing access it has allowed to both information about powerlifting as a sport and representations of a diverse range of people participating in it and using gym spaces. However, the process of mainstreaming seems to have begun far earlier than the advent of online platforms. Alan Klein, a professor of anthropology from Northeastern University in the USA, intensively documented the subculture of exclusive bodybuilding and powerlifting gyms like Gold's in the 1980s, which has since become internationally franchised:

There were a lot of people in bodybuilding who lamented the fact that it was becoming so popular. They liked it when it was a more meaningful community. They saw that people were pouring in in droves, but there was a time before Gold's Gym franchised, where you would not enter that gym unless you were a high-end competitor. There was a time when if I went across country, I could not find a gym at all unless it was a YMCA. Of course, today gyms are like mushrooms, they're everywhere. So there's that shift from a smaller niche sport to this larger thing, and that shift comes with a price. People who have been in that original community, they see the difference.

A major part of the mainstreaming of bodybuilding occurred with peer-to-peer information sharing through subscription-based bodybuilding magazines, Hollywood films and the growing popularity of at-home workout tapes by people like Jane Fonda. For some members of the older generation, the rapid growth of the gym industry, the mainstreaming and franchising of some of its formerly exclusive institutions, and the sudden proliferation of online coaching and content are viewed with a degree of suspicion. Formerly cloistered gym-based subcultures, Alan observed, provided a safe environment for obsessive, alienated and often traumatised men grappling with the impact of the decline of hegemonic white masculinity and postwar economic change in the United States of the 1970s and 1980s – around the same time that the Australian Institute of Sport was founded in response to Australia's national humiliation at the Montreal Olympics. Those stalwarts, whose relationships with each other, Alan notes in his 1993 study

Little Big Men, were ruled by unrestrained competitive impulses, intense dominance and submission dynamics, hustling and narcissistic psychologies, were incredibly defensive of their space. Alan comments that after the rapid mainstreaming of the sport through the impact of Hollywood and popular media 'the doors opened and everybody seemed to be able to get a gym membership at Gold's Gym. And I remember the guys grumbling.'

Despite the recent mainstream attention, powerlifters tend to maintain an elitist and outsider mindset. This status-obsessed mentality continues to attract new people to the sport. Alan noted when I interviewed him that at Gold's 'every now and then a powerlifter came in, and it was as if the sea had parted. Powerlifters were the real thing. And they had a tremendous status within the gym subculture.' One interviewee, Kat, a lifter who trains in Burwood, told me that 'If you are in the free weight section doing powerlifting, there's a certain kind of status attached.'

I ask Kat whether they think there is an incel element to this – meaning, is it possible that people are drawn to powerlifting because they feel they lack power, are alienated by culture at large and seeking to compensate for it.

'I really actually think that a lot of powerlifting is like that . . . That, I think, is what originally attracted me about it.'

Kat 'never really identified as someone who is sporty', but found themselves compelled by the social power of doing powerlifting in public gym spaces.

I speak to Bev Francis, star of the 1985 film *Pumping Iron II: The Women* and co-owner of the Bev Francis Powerhouse Gym, a long-running bodybuilding institution in New York, to get a better understanding of the mainstreaming effect. Bev has been in bodybuilding and powerlifting gyms since the 1970s. Originally a track and field athlete at the University of Melbourne, she, along with two other women in the team, was encouraged and 'invited to come into powerlifting', initially as part of her training regimen. Then she realised she was really good at it. 'It wasn't something that I chose. And there were basically no women apart from us.' Despite this lack of female representation, she felt welcomed.

At age sixty-eight, having left the sport in the 1980s to pursue bodybuilding, she returned to competition in 2021 and immediately set records in her age category. When she takes my call from her house in Geelong, where we both grew up, Bev has just completed the nine-day Great Victorian Bike Ride with her girlfriend. She is a thoughtful, open and critical conversation partner. She is well aware of, and seems resilient to, the controversy she generated with her unapologetically muscular body and extraordinary strength in the field of women's bodybuilding and powerlifting. She's aware of the fact that the film, and her particular role in it, continues to be talked about in university gender studies classrooms.

Bev and Steve, her business partner and ex-husband, have worked hard to make Bev's gym a place that can be both accessible to complete beginners and specialised enough for those who are deep in the culture. Her gym is intentionally 'a place that is not scary for a housewife to walk into because there's not big guys screaming and yelling and throwing weights around. So everyone's well behaved, everyone's friendly . . . as well as, you know, Mr Olympia might be training or some pro footballers, some celebrities, and that's a thrill as well.'

*

Sam Dengate, a trans man and the owner of boutique gym T Generation in Brunswick East, on Wurundjeri Country, has been one of the most determined drivers and advocates for trans self-organised sports participation in Australia. He was presented with a Victorian Pride Award in 2022 for outstanding contributions to sport after running a highly successful trans and non-binary powerlifting meet, the Trans Takeover, in November 2022. Sam struggles to keep up with the demand for his services; trans and non-binary people are desperate to be coached by someone they feel safe with and who understands their experience, and there are so few trans and non-binary people who have managed to stay in the fitness industry and make a living.

I'm interested in how good mentorship can encourage trans people to participate in sporting fields that they have been excluded from. Sam has chosen to embrace the parental element of mentorship as part of his branding: 'Coach Daddy, that is what all of the gym members have named me.' There is a natural draw towards this dynamic in communities that experience both a disconnect from their families of origin and an intergenerational disconnect within the LGBTIQA+ community. For Sam, this can be a productive basis for sports coaching, 'if you think about the concept of Daddy as the hand to hold and the foot in your arse when you need to pull your head in. I am happy doing that role.'

Kat tells me that their coach, another trans powerlifter from their gym, made sure that Kat approached their first competition with a positive mindset. While they'd been incredibly anxious, their coach encouraged them to focus on making connections with the other lifters and have fun. 'He had said to me, you know, be nice. I got a lot out of it, because that's what I went in with.'

Rory Lynch, an athlete and coach who lives in Warrane (Sydney) but grew up in Aotearoa's North Island, is a contributor to an online database of women and non-binary people in strength culture. They felt that the dominance of heterosexual male perspectives in the industry was a serious issue, and for that reason they actively sought out a female coach. Rory is very selective. They need their clients to be extremely dedicated and focused on self-improvement; those chosen few have to do what they've agreed to. But there is also an in-built element of care and responsibility. 'As a powerlifting coach, you need to care about people. That doesn't necessarily mean that you make decisions that they're going to like all the time, but the decisions that you make should be in their best interest all of the time.'

Sam believes there will be a greater push from crowds of trans people new to the sport who want to be able to compete in the field. The demand is already beginning to outstrip the preparedness of federations and service providers to cater for these new crowds, Sam says: 'As the interest builds, now we need to start really building these pathways.' Sam is pushing hard to create these opportunities, and for good reason. Trans people have become caught in the crossfire in the institutional battles over anti-doping and fairness in powerlifting, which have made the rules around competing more confusing.

In the years following his split from the IPF, Wilks talked openly and unrepentantly about the actions he'd taken. The rule of the IPF over powerlifting internationally was, he argued, 'deeply, profoundly, utterly corrupt' with regards to drug testing. In the United States, another rebellion from the IPF occurred in 2021 within USA Powerlifting (USAPL), the largest and most popular powerlifting federation in the United States. This split was also linked to the issue of doping, specifically the USAPL's non-compliance with the protocols of the World Anti-Doping Agency (WADA) code for testing athletes. The debate led to both sides implying that the other was potentially enabling drug cheats through a series of 'passive-aggressive social media posts and vague press releases'.

Even in the absence of Olympic participation, in a drug-tested competitive sport like powerlifting, compliance with WADA codes and the policies and rulings handed down by the IOC is linked to a sense of global legitimacy. Belonging to WADA affirms that a federation is playing the sport in its fairest and purest form. Even when Wilks split from the IPF, he maintained an ambition to increase powerlifting's status on the world stage and to build the profile of his own newly founded international federation, World Powerlifting (WP). With this in mind, WP maintained a strict adherence to the rulings of the IOC and of WADA on testing and on the inclusion of transgender athletes. The conditions set out in the IOC ruling of 2015 state that trans men can compete 'without restriction' as long as they comply with WADA's rules, which require obtaining a therapeutic use exemption for testosterone use. For trans women, there is a list of more specific rules, not only applied to hormone levels, but also scrutinising the legitimacy of how the athlete identifies.

WP's adherence to these rules is what enabled both me and Sam to compete alongside other men, albeit with some pretty inconvenient conditions we both had to meet regarding our testosterone use. Achieving a therapeutic use exemption requires regular testing to ensure the maintenance of a 'normal male level' of testosterone, which feels both arbitrary and unfairly applied, given no other men are required to submit to regular testing of their hormones. This annoyed Sam, but what bothered him more was the feeling of indignity in the ways he was talked through the application of this rule. 'It was very dismissive,' he said. 'It was like I'd been categorised as unthreatening, like, "it's not like you're gonna get national titles". I was like, well, fuck you, mate, let's go.'

By contrast, trans women are routinely subject to rhetoric that characterises them as potential cheaters and threats to women's sport. So the IOC rulings on trans inclusion do not provide a perfect system. They are one model that will inevitably continue fluctuating, and as Rory Lynch reflected, they are just seen as 'the fairest we have' based on the available science. But Jordan Feigenbaum, an online coach from California with a popular podcast and YouTube channel, authored a report on trans and intersex inclusion in sports in 2019, which proposes that the temptation to 'rely on science' as the main factor in decision-making obscures the fact that increased participation of all people in sports is a social good. For Jordan (who crossed over from a career in medicine to coaching and fitness influencing), coming from a public health advocacy perspective, this is too often ignored when it should be central.

In contrast to PA and the APU, the USAPL rejected the legitimacy and authority of the IOC altogether and, significantly, it acted to ban trans people from competition in 2018. This was a direct rejection of the IOC ruling of 2015 that provided guidelines for the participation of trans athletes. The USAPL's subsequent ousting from the IPF in 2021 on the basis that it wasn't following WADA protocols to the letter allowed it to position the IPF as corrupt, authoritarian and ineffective. USAPL could then fashion itself as a renegade moral champion of anti-doping, of the athletes and of the 'real sport'. It then established an 'Mx' category, excluding all trans people from the gendered competition and forcing them to compete in a separate category.

The USAPL's departure from the IPF also prompted it to seek to internationalise, as Wilks had done with World Powerlifting, and it has succeeded in making itself very attractive to Australian audiences. At the time, Australian powerlifters were grappling with the downfall of PA as their main organising power structure. They were searching for alternative federations that would meet their needs as competitors and lovers of the sport while also fostering a more positive value system. It was at this time that the USAPL, fresh from the scandal of its own departure from the IPF, opened its new franchise USAPL Australia. Australian lifters – seemingly unaware of, or unbothered by, the last three years of scandal in the USAPL over trans exclusion, anti-doping and other controversial rules it had taken an extremely rigid approach to enforcing – appear to have jumped on board at all levels, from novice lifters to the advanced. USAPL is now cementing itself as a serious competitor of the IPF-affiliated APU. So, if you are a trans or non-binary person competing in powerlifting in Australia, you now have two completely different options: to be out and compete in the USAPL as Mx, or to comply with the restrictions and paperwork demanded by WADA and compete in the APU as a man or a woman.

For some athletes, the USAPL provides an attractive glitz and showiness that the more serious and sterile IPF federations don't match. One newer lifter in competition prep, Justine, who also trains in Naarm, noted that the production of USAPL meets felt geared towards increasing a glamorous social media presence for the sport, which would draw in both new athletes and big money. 'The performance is a big part of it . . . everything's really tightly curated. But one thing that I didn't like in the contract they gave me is that you have to agree to your image being used, so they can photograph you and use your image for promo.'

Treating powerlifting meets (which often run for hours and are famously not all that exciting to watch) as a form of sports entertainment requires a bit of extra effort to engage audiences. Other lifters in Australia who have remained with the APU are sceptical about the USAPL's ability to effectively raise the profile of the sport. Rory Lynch noted that the multiplication of competing federations, all using their own scoring systems, rules and weight classes, means that 'the depth of competition is not there. What I would really like to see is one tested federation and one untested federation. I think that would result in a better competitive environment.' Powerlifters, especially those at a higher level, tend to have a strong desire for a uniform ranking system that can reliably predict who is the best, a scoring system that can successfully rank superiority across differences. Adding the USAPL to the mix in the Australian field muddies these waters.

The USAPL's trans ban appeared to be its first hint of explicit disagreement with the IPF. Although it hasn't been verified, there are suspicions among some former USAPL members that its refusal to budge on the trans ban, conflicting with the IPF's decision to accept the IOC ruling in 2015, was a key issue in their eventual split. Whether or not this is true, the USAPL stood firm in its decision to maintain the ban to an extent that some found bizarre in its rigidity. This was despite fierce debates on the evidentiary basis for that ban, a number of protests at local and state level meets, and lifters abandoning it for other, more inclusive federations.

Janae Marie Kroc, from Michigan in the United States, is one of those who abandoned the USAPL. She is a unique figure in world powerlifting. Following a career in the US Marines, including a period when she served under Bill Clinton in presidential security, she became a highly successful world champion powerlifter. She achieved a world record in the male 220lb (100kg) weight class in the WPO federation in 2006 at the Arnold Classic sports festival and gathered a huge following of fans and supporters over the thirteen years she was involved in the sport. Then, in 2015, she publicly came out to the powerlifting community as a gender fluid trans woman.

Janae was the first, and remains the only, powerlifter to achieve a major sponsorship, which effectively made her a career powerlifter. Sponsorship at this level had previously been awarded to high-level bodybuilders and a handful of elite Strongman competitors who worked as advocates for large multinational supplement brands, but never to a powerlifter. 'I received a monthly salary, they flew me all over, and I was treated more like the top bodybuilders were, given a lot of exposure,' Janae says. 'I was with them for eight years.'

This level of income and prestige for lifting and competing at a high level is hard to comprehend for an average powerlifter in Australia, many of whom might pay hundreds of dollars per year just to be allowed to compete in local level competition. But Janae's pre-transition self, Matt Kroc the marine, was the perfect symbol for the hypermasculine branding of MuscleTech, a multinational supplement company. 'At the time, they were one of, if not the biggest, supplement company in the world. They had an economy line that was carried by companies like Walmart. They were doing something like $800 million a year in business.'

While Janae was a representative of MuscleTech, it was achieving incredible success in the American and global markets alongside competitors like Optimum Nutrition and BSN, and its recruitment of top athletes in many popular sports was key in helping it reach a wide audience.

I interview Janae over video call; she's in a crowded office in her gym in Michigan. I can hear people working out just beyond the door, and I feel as though I can picture exactly what's going on out there. She describes it to me, sounding happy. The gym caters to a wide audience, but it is still very powerlifting focused. They have a set-up that includes wrestling mats, a 20-metre strip of turf, cardio equipment and heavy bags, as well as a pool table in the lobby that is very popular. 'I compete in jujitsu now, so you'll see me and my training partners in here rolling on the mats. I built the gym that I always wanted and then hoped other people would like it too.'

When Janae came out to her fans and followers as trans after being outed by a YouTuber, the reaction was intense. 'It was quite a shock, I'm sure . . . I was known as this Ultimate Alpha Male, which is definitely an aspect of my personality,' she told Rover Radio in an interview. In 2015, at a sports event where MuscleTech had a stall set up, a powerlifter who had heard online rumours about Janae being trans approached its representative to ask why it would support her. 'They basically said, you know, Matt Kroc is trans, in a very negative way, and why are you guys supporting this person?'

Afraid of the damage this could do to the brand, MuscleTech terminated its agreement with Janae almost immediately. 'They said, "You've been removed from the website . . . we'll pay you through the end of your contract in December, but for all intents and purposes, you're done with MuscleTech."' Janae recognised this as an impersonal, commercially driven position, and still regards the relationships she had with the employees at MuscleTech as positive. She isn't sure whether there would have been the same outcome with the sponsorship had she come out today – like Sam, she acknowledges that there has been a culture shift around gender identity in sports in the USA and Australia, which has been rapid and far reaching. But it's clear that even with Janae's ability to understand the context and empathise with the company's position, this decision would have been extremely hurtful, not to mention damaging for her career and livelihood.

Janae had been tossing up whether to publicly transition for years. Her powerlifting career was complicating her desires to change her body and publicly articulate her femininity within her community and industry. Her transition efforts before 2015 had been limited to privately disclosing her status to her family and friends, and trying to diet down to a smaller frame in an effort to look more feminine in public. But losing her muscles wasn't something she was prepared to do: 'I wasn't done with my powerlifting career yet.' She recognises now that while there is a long way to go, there has been a culture shift in gender norms regarding how muscular women are viewed.

Janae was a legendary competitor as a man and remains a skilled athlete. Hers is a case that no cisgender sporting body is ready to confront: a trans woman who wants to compete at a high level and refuses to comply with the demand that trans women in sports be demure, small or non-competitive. She is doggedly, terrifyingly strong, hard-working and motivated to win. On top of this, she has done a lot to elevate the profile of powerlifting and to open its doors to new markets: 'I'm the best bargain MuscleTech has ever got.

I was paid less than the bodybuilders and it ended up working out really well for [MuscleTech]. I worked really hard.'

The intensity of the backlash experienced by Janae is one example of what can happen when a trans person lives fully in their own identity while staying dedicated to their sport. A friend of Janae's, Bucky Motter, the head of the International Association of Trans Bodybuilders and Powerlifters, reflects on the violence of the response to her public revelation that she was trans. 'People were burning the posters of Matt Kroc. They just went nuts, almost paramilitary,' he recalls.

I ask Janae whether she felt there was a fascist element to the backlash. 'There definitely is. I think that's part of the culture of the country as a whole right now,' she says.

Sam Dengate's main clientele are trans and non-binary people who typically find gyms a challenging, frightening place. The Trans Takeover provided Sam with a way to teach a few of them how powerlifting meets run and to give them an opportunity to participate in organised sport for the first time. 'About 70 per cent of the lifters there had never competed in a sport, ever, due to issues like lack of access, prejudice and fear.' While so much of the focus and debate on trans people's participation in sport tends to fixate on the possibility of trans inclusion perverting the fairness of sport at the elite level, this is an important reminder that a vast majority of trans people struggle to gain entry to sports at all due to the social and political barriers they face.

Sam doesn't want patronising, partial inclusion on cisgender society's terms. He and his clients want not only to be allowed to play within the existing structures, but to see their community celebrated and fully bring themselves to that sporting culture. Not only that, the trans community wants the ability to compete and to be excellent in the sport. Sam, for that reason, was extremely frustrated by the terms of inclusion set out for him in Powerlifting Australia. 'I was like, fuck that,' he tells me. 'I'll do it myself, then.'

The IOC released a new inclusion framework partly aimed at addressing trans participation in 2021. That report contextualises its recommendations within what it acknowledges as a highly divisive political debate on trans participation, a demand to address harm done to athletes, and a lack of scientific consensus on testosterone and the advantages it may or may not confer. One of its most striking statements is that there must be no presumption of advantage due to trans status or sex variations without solid, verifiable evidence.

In March 2023, a series of rallies against trans rights, specifically targeting trans women, were held in Australia and Aotearoa, one of which was attended by neo-Nazis in support of its message. During the same week, World Athletics (WA), an international governing body for track and field sports, moved to ban both trans women who had gone through 'any stage' of male puberty, and athletes with differences in sex development (also known as intersex) who have a plasma testosterone limit of over 2.5nmol, half the previous allowable limit. The ban extended only to elite competition, in a field where there are no transgender athletes currently active at that tier at all. Alongside that ban, WA also announced its intention to set up a working group led by a transgender athlete that would be dedicated to the issue of trans inclusion. Observing all of this reaffirmed a belief I have that fascist systems and insipid, ineffective performances of inclusivity can coexist. Sports have always been a staging ground for both.

Born a Catholic, Raised a Catholic: Why I No Longer Practise My Faith

Introduction by
Amanda Hooton

Claire works so hard. I did not expect this. For starters, she's too glamorous, surely? When I was her age I was turning up to work at the newspaper in my Ugg boots and pyjamas; she is interviewing Paul Rudd in her red-carpet dress and doing a million pieces to camera every twenty-four hours. She's also too young. Most under-thirty-year-olds I hear about are refusing to work weekends and worrying about their work-life balance; Claire sometimes texts me at 9 am on Saturday and has clearly been slogging away for several hours. And she is, after all, a Gen Z. Long-form journalism is nasty and brutish and long, so long. As an act of creation, it's hard to think of anything that takes more effort and provides less instant gratification, less guaranteed success, or a less obviously apprecia-tive audience. Why on earth would anyone born after 1990 bother?

Still, it's so thrilling to watch when somebody does. Especially someone with so many strings to her bow, so many other ways to tell stories. Each time I edited her writing I wondered if she'd take my suggestions: would she make the phone calls, check the details, do the exhausting nuts-and-bolts thinking that a long story demands? But who knew – beneath the glamour, beneath the twenty-something, happy-go-lucky smile lurked the stone heart of a writer. I think it nearly killed her calling the priest – it would have nearly killed me. But she knew the story needed it, and when I read the next version, there it was, done.

Whatever the news desk tells you, first-person stories are the hardest of all to write. There is nowhere to hide, nothing to mediate your connection to readers. You invite them in, and you must engage them one on one and answer their questions, or fail completely. Claire kept answering my questions, and asking her own. She kept her grace, her sense of humour and her own voice: the three qualities most often lost in the editing maw. She could, it's quite clear to me, do anything, and probably will. But long-form would be lucky to have her.

Born a Catholic, Raised a Catholic: Why I No Longer Practise My Faith

Claire Keenan

CONTENT WARNING: THIS ARTICLE CONTAINS REFERENCES TO SEXUAL ASSAULT AND CHILD ABUSE.

IT'S 2008, ON A SUNDAY MORNING, AND I AM WHERE I'M ALWAYS meant to be: praying for the forgiveness of my sins and for ultimate delivery. I'm sitting, like I do every Sunday, on an uncomfortable pew engraved with the initials (not mine: I would be instantly in trouble) of hundreds of previously bored children. It creaks whenever its occupants stand.

On this Sunday, like every Sunday, I'm drifting off into my own little world, staring at the ornate ceiling painted a sickly baby blue. If you follow the arc of this ceiling to the point above the altar, you'll see fluffy white clouds painted like a gateway to heaven – all creamy and dreamy. Out of the three churches my family attends, this is by far my favourite, because of the ceiling, and because of the stations of the cross that have 3D wooden Jesuses leaning out of them, complete with kneeling disciples and weeping women all around Him.

Just like where the thorny woven crown pierces the side of His skull, bright blood trickles out of the nails puncturing His palms. It used to scare me, but once I was taught He died for us so we could all go to heaven, it seemed less scary – oddly reassuring, even.

However lurid the decorative details, nothing dramatic ever happens in church. Each Sunday is just like every other Sunday: a vague old white man speaking to my easily distracted siblings and me. Until today. Today, I notice that the rustle from latecomers taking their seats, the muffled laughter as kids elbow each other for attention, has suddenly stopped. I turn my head to see a broad, handsome Samoan man dressed in priest's robes coming slowly up the aisle, fist-pumping the latecomers and brooding teens, green stole flowing behind him like he's on a catwalk, his smile big and wide and twinkling. My cousin's knuckles, a few rows back, brush the knuckles of this stranger – my eyebrows rise as if he's just touched someone famous.

Reaching the altar, the apparition turns. 'In the name of the Father, and of the Son and of the Holy Spirit.'

The sign of the cross is made in unison, as we respond: 'Amen.'

'The grace of our Lord Jesus Christ, and the love of God and the communion of the Holy Spirit be with you,' he says to the crowd, still smiling.

We respond: 'And with your spirit.'

Did I just hear extra enthusiasm in the words, his and ours? I stare, sensing warmth and kindness in this man in robes, something I haven't really felt before. I watch him closely through the first and second readings (read by my aunty: my family are among the regular speakers, whichever church we're at) until he is delivering the Gospel reading, and finally the homily. Usually a time set aside for me to muse about my latest boy crush, this week the new priest's sermon actually makes the audience laugh. It's like a modern miracle! People are turning, looking at each other in surprise. Are they thinking what I'm thinking: *Is this man for real? And if so, who brought him here? Jesus himself?*

It was the weekly promise of hot cinnamon donuts from the local Donut King that generally brought my siblings and me to church every Sunday. Pushed on by Mum and Dad, the four of us would pile out of the house and into our golden Honda Odyssey – the only one in our town (the small and mighty Griffith, in Wiradjuri Country) – so people knew, *always*, where the Keenans were going. The same well-dressed families would be in attendance every week: the Kennedys, the McAllisters, the De Valentins, the Ryans.

Once I was old enough to stay with the adults for the whole mass (graduating from the children's liturgy run by the mothers with their finely trimmed super-mum bob haircuts – mine included), giving the sign of peace was by far my favourite ritual. It was the penultimate moment when we, the audience, broke the fourth wall between each other, turning away from the priest to shake our neighbours' hands and say 'Peace be with you'. Somehow it made me feel extra important, almost equal to the adults, like I had the same amount of peace to give. It was also the sign that mass was close to ending. A last burst of energy would zap through me as I tried to shake as many big hands as I could before: 'Lamb of God, you take away the sins of the world, have mercy on us.'

As a young journalist, I've reported on the overthrow of Roe v Wade, victim-survivor stories, the banning of gay conversion therapy and – tediously – the religious discrimination bill before parliament. Not once have I written about my own religious story, never considering my own spiritual journey, or its questions, its silences, its uncertainties and, admittedly, its denials.

Am I Catholic today? Technically: yes. Once a person is baptised, they are forever Catholic, or so I'm told. It runs in our bloodlines. In my day-to-day life? Definitely not. I mean, of the values, yes, but the actual practice, no. Lately, though, I've been thinking about who stays Catholic and who doesn't – and why I didn't. Why am I no longer Catholic today?

Whatever the reasons, I'm certainly not alone. As reported by the Australian Bureau of Statistics, Christianity as a whole in Australia has fallen by almost 10 per cent in the last five years.[1] 'This is the year Australia stops being a Christian nation,' Dr Mark Stephens of the Centre for Public Christianity wrote in 2021[2], and boy, was he bang on. Today less than half of all Australians are practising Christians. Which prompts the question: why?

One quick and obvious answer is that people have turned away from Christianity as a result of the abuse scandals. The Catholic church in particular is now synonymous with child sex abuse, something that is both historically and presently devastating, and deeply traumatic for its subjects. The church's handling of such cases has been, arguably, equally traumatising, with delays, denials and refusals to acknowledge its responsibility to victims. But in my own town, in which such a scandal would strike at the very heart

1   'Religious Affiliation in Australia', 4 July 2022, based on 'Cultural diversity: Census, 2021', Australian Bureau of Statistics, viewed 27 January 2023.
2   Stephens, Mark, 'Has Australia Lost Its Religion, or Merely Its Affection for Institutions?', *Sydney Morning Herald*, 5 August 2021.

of our church community and involve none other than our own beloved, warm, fist-pumping priest – Father Neru – it didn't cause a wholesale flight from the church, by either the town's faithful or my own family. Not even, perhaps, by me.

Today there are only around 5 million Catholics practising in Australia. Mind you, that's still 20 per cent of the population, making Catholicism the largest religious denomination in the country. On the flip side, 10 million people reported having no religion at all in the 2021 census, and this number rises year on year.

There is, moreover, a knock-on effect: as fewer families have religion in their lives, fewer children are exposed to it. Thirty-year-old Nathan Costin is the campus ministry manager at the Australian Catholic University. 'If you're not in a family or a community where faith is important, how else are you going to encounter it?' he asks. 'When you're talking about religion and you're talking about faith, by its nature, it is very deep. It requires contemplation, it requires thinking, it affects the whole aspect of your life.'

I certainly encountered it in my own family, as did my siblings. Extremely privileged, we come from a close, loving, faithful family, a nun in our extended family, as well as a priest, multitudes of Catholic teachers (even a principal), and many pillars of the church community – invisible guardians cleaning, arranging flowers, printing pamphlets and performing the countless tasks that keep local churches running. We had a Catholic education, all throughout schooling – my cousins as well. And yet today, like me, none of my siblings are religious, despite the fact we could not have had a more faithful start to our lives.

*

Long before any discussion of what I should be called, everybody knew I was to be baptised. Just like my brother and sister before me, I would be draped in white like a mini-bride and holy water would be poured on my tiny forehead. Photos would be taken, printed and carefully placed in my very own album, a kind of sacrament scrapbook lovingly and dutifully prepared by my mother for all four of her children. Over the phone, Mum tells me she can't find a photo from my First Reconciliation, the sacrament after baptism. All I recall is my seven-year-old self with sweaty palms trying to think of a sin to tell the priest – in my own mind I was the optimal child. And then there I am at eight, for my First Holy Communion, grinning in a turquoise knitted cardigan, long brown skirt covered up by a white gown and wooden cross. And at eleven, there I am in a pretty pink dress for my confirmation, which Mum drove three and a half hours to Albury Myer to buy for me.

What baffles me now, swiping through the digitally sent pictures, is that this little girl used to bow her head passionately and recite 'Our Father' when told to, she served the bread and wine as a Eucharist minister in high school, once taught how to, and kissed the six-foot statue of Blessed Virgin Mary at the front of her grandparents' garden just because she wanted to. 'You just do the rituals, and then it becomes real, even if you don't [initially] believe in it. That's what religion is,' says Honor Levy[3], a Catholic convert and writer who lives in the United States. I did the rituals, I did believe. And then, somehow, I didn't.

---

3   Yost, Julia, 'New York's Hottest Club Is the Catholic Church', *The New York Times*, 9 August 2022.

If I reflect on my own faith collapsing, it all feels, strangely, quite seamless and natural. Once I saw what else was out there in the world, I couldn't bring myself to sit and recite words I didn't fully believe in back to a priest. 'I believe in one God, the Father almighty, maker of heaven and earth.' Sure, I hoped there was a heaven, but did one man really die for all our sins? And who got to decide what a sin is? How could God judge a young woman for wanting to be touched and loved by anyone she pleased, especially outside of marriage? How could sexual and individualistic exploration be a sin?

Nearly ten years after I stopped being a Catholic, in my own mind at least, I find myself standing nervously outside my grandma's house. Usually I am not this way. Usually I am racing to get inside to sit and chat with her. Today, though, I want to finally ask her about our priest, that priest we all adored. You see, if I reflect on why I stopped believing in God, I enter a tug of war with myself over what was going on in the mind of a teenage girl: boys, school, work, boys. But nothing had occurred in my life that would, on the face of it, make me fundamentally question my faith. Except for that priest – the one who made coming to church exciting. Eight years ago, that priest was arrested for allegedly raping a child.

'It was very upsetting for us,' my grandmother tells me. It is November 2022, the day of her eightieth birthday, and Grandma is dressed in one of her iconic swirl-patterned jumpers with diamantes, and a white-collared shirt sitting stylishly underneath – I say iconic because she has the same in almost every colour. Today it is aqua. 'John wasn't alive when that all happened. It would've upset him terribly because they were very close.'

John is my grandad, the Irish Catholic patriarch on my

father's side, who played a big role in our faith – and in the local village parish. Alongside my grandma, he helped with the upkeep of the church and in my mind probably could've been a priest himself, if he hadn't met and fallen in love with my beautiful grandma. A marriage certificate signed by Pope Paul VI has hung on their bedroom wall for decades.

I remember quite clearly where I was when I first read the news about Father Neru. It was a Friday in November 2015, and I was seventeen, at boarding school, sitting cross-legged on my bed, my Dell laptop resting hotly on my thighs, my school dress crumpled in the middle. There was a statue of Mother Mary staring up at me through the window. She stood, poetically (a prima madonna), next to the oak tree where we boarders sat every lunchtime, serving as a physical, in-your-face reminder of what good little Catholic girls should be. The dorms were loud and busy with excited weekend traffic when I read the ABC headline: 'Community shock at arrest of popular Catholic priest on child sexual assault charge'.[4] It was a real jolt to the stomach.

My parents were shocked too, obviously. I must have spoken about it to them, either on the phone or at home during the holidays, but I don't remember many words – just that there weren't many words to say. At the age of forty-nine, Father Neru Leuea was charged with a historical aggravated sexual assault of a girl under the age of sixteen. It was alleged that the assault occurred between 2002 and 2003, around the time Father Neru first began working as a priest in Griffith, when the alleged victim was just ten years old, and five years before I met him.

---

4   'Shock at popular priest's arrest in Narrandera', ABC News, 12 November 2015.

At his 2016 trial at the Wagga District Court, Father Neru pleaded not guilty. Before I even ask Grandma how she felt when the arrest happened, she explains that he told her one day, 'I've got proof, Lesley. I wasn't even in the country when she claims that.' It's her way of saying innocent without actually saying it. I nod, not wanting to upset her. The entire town had said it over the years, confident the person making the claims had lied to try to bring Father down. 'He had such an influence on young people,' she goes on. 'He was a people's priest. He never crossed a line where he shouldn't have.' I was a young person, and she's right. He did have an influence on us. He was our . . . the town's priest.

Father Neru was acquitted in October 2016, in a judge-alone trial. Presiding judge Gordon Lerve couldn't confirm beyond reasonable doubt that an offence had occurred within the time-frame. That was that. Father Neru was moved away from the diocese, my parents attended church with a new priest, and my siblings and I began splitting our lives between the dust of home and city boarding schools and universities. When I later learned that only 1–10 per cent of allegations of sexual assault are estimated to be false, I thought of the case. When I read Facebook comments[5] from my town's Catholic residents, filled with red-hot iron anger because Father Neru was still forbidden to practise as a priest, I felt in opposition, discredited. A couple of years later, when I was living overseas, I would think of the case once more when the person I was dating confided in me that he had been sexually abused by a Catholic figure as a child. I had no answers to give him, only love

---

5 Facebook post, Griffith Free Local News, 2019. Available at: facebook.com/griffithfreelocalnews/posts/catholic-priest-father-neru-leuea-who-was-acquitted-of-a-child-sex-offence-but-a/852087761791020/, viewed 10 October 2022.

and support. No certainty about any of it. But isn't certainty something that religion, unlike the rest of life, is actually supposed to give?

In 2021, Australian author and social commentator Monica Dux wrote *Lapsed*, an entire book about no longer being a practising Catholic. In it, she wanted to answer two questions: 'Is there something special about Catholics, a shared identity, one that bleeds into us lapsed as well? And if there is, what should we do about it?'[6]

During Christmas of 2022, *Lapsed* became my bible for the holidays, that time of year when summer feels like it could stretch out forever, as long as a country backyard hose. Accompanied by Monica's book, I talked to young Catholics who had found answers to their questions, maintained their certainty and kept their faith while I had lost mine. Along the way, I found fellow lapsed people, eager to share stories of their faith collapsing.

I speak to 29-year-old clean energy specialist Tom the same week Cardinal George Pell dies. The controversial Catholic figure is a dividing point in his family, he tells me. Tom is lanky and friendly, and has a blond moustache and a hooped earring in his right ear. We end up chatting for well over an hour. During Pell's trial, Tom's family group chat lit up with 'Fuck, George Pell is the worst' from Tom or his siblings, whereupon Tom's dad would reply with a simple 'Withholding comment', quietly confident that Pell would win. 'My dad is a very staunch arch-conservative Catholic,

6   Dux, Monica, *Lapsed*, ABC Books, 2021, p. 299.

who voted no to same sex marriage [another divisive church issue, if we're keeping score] and convinced my mum to vote no as well,' Tom explains. Growing up, the family would attend church every weekend, say grace before meals and recite the rosary while travelling. Did he truly believe in God as a kid? Tom laughs and says, 'A hundred per cent, because there was no alternative. That was the reality we lived in.' I smile knowingly.

Unlike Tom's family, my parents never questioned why all four of their children stopped going to mass once we hit our twenties. There was no family meeting about it, only special-occasion hassles – Easter and Christmas – but even they have become more relaxed with time, age and hangovers.

Tom and his siblings were culturally Catholic for a long time, but now Tom refuses to attend even special-occasion services. 'One of the things which upsets me is that I had no agency in my religion,' he says. 'It was a thing imposed on me. And [when I began to have doubts] my dad would ask me questions like, "Why are you abandoning God?" rather than "What pushed you away from the church?"'

What if the answer to this question – what pushed you away? – is the church's own teaching, telling you your entire existence is a sin? Samuel Martin, a thirty-year-old trans person, grew up in an ultra-religious family in Kempsey and then in Brisbane/Meanjin. Sam's grandfather is a pastor, and before Sam transitioned, he identifed as gay, which wasn't the 'lifestyle' his single mother wanted for her eldest child. In what feels truly unfair, and even cruel, Sam also attended Citipointe Christian school – now infamous for its contract enforcing parents to enrol their students only on the basis of their biological sex.

Overcoming the suffering caused by his religious upbringing and his education, including not speaking to his family anymore, Sam is finally living his true self. We chat on Zoom, Sam in his happy place – the gym. He is grinning and bearing his self-made muscles. Sam believes that if people are living a life that aligns with their own values, then they may no longer need religion. 'You are the only person that can get yourself out of bed every day,' he says. 'God doesn't do that for you.'

Even in the days of my belief, God never got me out of bed. My mum did that. Who in recent years, though my family still doesn't discuss religion all that much, and even though both my parents are loyal members of the church (Mum more so than Dad), has had the ability to preserve a healthy distance, a critical eye on the church. Before lockdown, Mum switched churches because her usual priest was using his homilies to spread anti-vax messaging. Maybe this is why our family has avoided the conflict and heartache of Tom's and Sam's. My parents have given us their values of love, acceptance, forgiveness and tolerance – which are (mostly) shared by the church – and yet none of those values have made us truly believe.

During 2021 and 2022, Sydney hosted Australia's Plenary Council for the first time in eighty years. It's the highest formal gathering of all local Catholic churches in the country, where bishops (and, in a recent addition, lay members) vote on the direction of the church, for the entire country. A rising feminist star of the most recent meeting was 26-year-old Madeline Forde, who is desperately trying to change the church's archaic view on women. A task I couldn't imagine ever doing.

We meet for coffee one Saturday morning on Glebe Point Road in Sydney (land of the Gadigal people of the Eora Nation). Maddy, dressed in a flowy Aboriginal art dress, is a paradox. She looks like a sweeter, more gentle version of me – as if God had upped his dosage of spirituality for her (I blink twice to see if there's a tiny yellow halo glowing above her head). And yet she is also much tougher and instantly more forthright than I have ever been. I think I am jealous of her.

At the council meeting, Maddy spoke up for the rights of women to be treated equally in the church. And then, meta- phorically speaking, all hell broke loose. '[My comments] got published in newspapers, I got backlash; I got told essentially you're not Catholic enough to be in this space. You don't have enough knowledge,' she says, shaking her head.

The two motions at the plenary council to change the role of women within the church both failed. Today, the church's hierarchy remains at odds with her beliefs in equality and LGBTQIA+ rights. But Maddy's not giving up. As well as being an Oceania representa- tive on the International Youth Advisory Body to the Vatican, she is a senior advisor for Catholic education in Adelaide. 'I'm not going to make myself smaller, I'm going to continue to amplify the voices of young women and people. If you look at the stories of the gospel, Jesus was someone who said, regardless of who you are, you are welcomed and you are loved. It's very clear that people have been discriminated against by the church. And it breaks my heart that it's still happening. We are all God's children.'

Perhaps if I'd witnessed someone willing to challenge the church's hierarchy and stubbornness around gender, identity and sexuality, I might have felt more inclined or supported as a teenager to stay within the faith. Or if I'd had someone like Father Bony Abraham around. He's a parish priest in the small town of Warwick (Gooragooby). The forty-year-old, who came to Australia from India in 2004, has impressively expanded Warwick's local Catholic church's attendees to include people below the age of fifty, and has even kickstarted a church youth group. He's a local superstar, and the young people feel it. Even *I* feel it over our grainy Zoom call.

'Young people feel when the church isn't participating with them,' he tells me. 'We want young people to take leadership in the church. Without them, the church doesn't really exist.' When I question why, in this case, the church won't do more for women and the LGBTQIA+ community, particularly for trans people like Sam, he answers with a question. 'The church is more powerful than Christ. The church is more demanding than Christ. And sometimes I wonder, is it Christ we are trying to hold on to? Or is it just the church's rules and regulations?'

Sabrina Stevens is a 31-year-old Kuku Yalanji and Yidinji woman born and raised in Cairns, home to the Yirrganydji people. Her great-grandmother was a part of the Stolen Generation, in which the Catholic church, of course, actively participated in the forced separation of children from their families and culture. 'The abhorrent practice of removing Aboriginal and Torres Strait Islander children . . . will remain forever a blight on our nation,' acknowledged the Catholic bishops of Australia in a formal statement in 1996, the first apology of its kind in this country.

To describe Sabrina is to describe a lioness; there's great gentleness and force to this woman, who is loyal to her mob and admired by her peers. Her Indigenous spirituality deeply connects her to the air she breathes and to the ground she walks on, especially while on Country. It seems impossible, given her family history, that she should want anything to do with the Catholic church. And yet, as we speak, I realise that where Sabrina stands today is literally right inside the institution that, in many people's eyes, betrayed her great-grandmother.

'My faith journey and my relationship within the Catholic church is never just my own journey,' explains Sabrina. 'It's always something that's been generational.' Sabrina's great-grandmother, incredibly, remained engaged within the Catholic church; her daughter (Sabrina's grandmother's sister) helped establish the National Aboriginal and Torres Strait Islander Catholic Council (NATSICC). Sabrina herself has been the youth counsellor at NATSICC for the past ten years, as well as a youth engagement officer at Caritas Australia, which is part of the international aid organisation of the Catholic Church.

Via this extraordinary sisterhood, the Catholic faith has remained strong in Sabrina's family, no matter how tainted its introduction. As a child, Sabrina attended Aboriginal mass, where the altar cloths were dotted with Aboriginal paintings, hymns and songs were sung in Language, and the Eucharist was brought up in a coolamon. 'I feel lucky to have found a way to connect my Catholic faith to my Aboriginal spirituality,' she explains. 'I know that's a unique space to be in, and I understand I'm very, very lucky to have that as part of my journey.'

Sabrina's is a profoundly personal experience: paradoxically complicated, wherein multiple truths exist at once. For her family at least, a trauma that should never have happened brought forward a rich religious faith that wouldn't have otherwise arrived. 'If you ask somebody what their faith journey is, it's always so unique to them,' she concludes. 'And I think that that's where the beauty lies.'

When I visit Sister Kathleen at her home in Canberra, the sound of my car brings her immediately to the front door, where she waves and opens the flyscreen. It's still summer, the air is as hot as a dryer, and I'm still driving around with my copy of Monica's book in the passenger seat. It doesn't know yet that a complete copy of the Bible will be sitting in its place when I leave Canberra.

Aunty Kath, as I know her, is my late grandad's sister. She's been a nun with the Sisters of Mercy for more than fifty years, but growing up I always knew her as the funny, albeit sometimes scary great-aunt. At seventy-seven, she's a firecracker, but not scary at all. A whole head shorter than me, she dresses primly in pants and a shirt – no habit since Vatican II. She wears glasses, and her greyish hair is cut short. When she was twenty she left her job, savings and motorbike to don the black-and-white habit of the Griffith convent. 'I always knew I wanted to give my life to Jesus Christ, to follow his way,' she says.

But she's surprisingly non-judgemental about other people's choices, mine included. 'If any person lives a fulfilled life of kindness and goodness to their neighbour and themselves, that's what Christ wants for us.' She pauses, then pulls a small yellow Bible out of a bag and hands it to me. 'It's all in here,' she says seriously. 'That's what the truth is all about.'

Yellow bibles aside, is the church doing enough to attract young people? I wonder.

She's visibly annoyed by my question. 'What would you like the church to do? Come on. Do young people need a concert every time they attend mass? Yes, the church could do more, but it's very hard to compete with the secular world.'

This is a common argument for why the church is losing members, and it's certainly valid – it's the argument that played out in my own life, after all: the enticements and questions and complexities of the secular world. But maybe it's easy to under-estimate the power of the religious world. Maddy and Sabrina have not stayed in the church for its entertainment value. They don't need a concert. Like Aunty Kath, they stayed for something else.

Following his acquittal in 2016, Father Neru was put on sabbatical by the bishop. This is what Grandma tells me when I call her to ask for his number. I imagine her flicking through her phone diary, standing in a long nightgown under her yellowy kitchen light. The last of the sun must be cut off by the red brick houses through her back window by now. She gives me the number. The warm evening air on my end tickles my body with sweat as I pace my balcony back and forth with each ring.

As soon as he begins to speak, I'm transported back to when I last saw him, ten years ago. He's saying mass for my grandparents' seventieth in my backyard, some years before the trial. There are hired white tables and chairs, tablecloths to match, wine in a proper chalice, Eucharist in a proper ciborium, all squished under a crisp marquee. I had totally forgotten this memory until now. I had forgotten my family: laughing, chatting, then respectfully silent for the blessing. And I had forgotten Father Neru, familiar and beaming at the head of our table.

These days Father Neru lives in Mulwala (Yorta Yorta lands) on the border of Victoria. He's still not allowed to be a priest. My grandmother recalls that Father Neru told her that for him to become a priest again, let alone run a parish, permission had to come all the way from Rome. Instead, he golfs. There's that warmth in his voice, just as I remember, which makes asking whether he's been back to Griffith since the trial feel extremely awkward. 'Oh yes, multiple times,' he says, surprisingly. He even blessed Grandma's new place when she moved in. This warmth remains even as he declines to give any quotes or comments about young people and the church. And before I get the chance to ask him explicitly about his trial or acquittal he has to go: he's cooking dinner, he tells me.

Thinking back on this conversation, there's a strange normalcy to it all. And yet I'm left reeling. The possible truth didn't leave my mouth; it couldn't fall out, knowing full well I would never know the exact truth. What I do know now, however, is that there are very few things that have made me as happy over the last six months as talking to my grandma on the phone so regularly. Since Grandad's passing, daily prayers have been her lifeline through grief. And in all of my life, at least, she's been the same quiet prayerful person she is today. She's never lost faith, and that faith is all encompassing.

All faith is profoundly personal. That doesn't mean we can't watch from the outside – a slow-moving ship, stable and steady, moving through uneven waters – appreciate its beauty and direction and think of what could've been if you'd stayed on board. On the dwindling numbers of young people staying with the church, Sabrina wonders why we need statistics for spirituality: 'When I'm doing youth work, I don't go out to get five new young people to sign up to the Catholic church every week. For me, it's more about creating a relationship with people and meeting them wherever they are.'

At this moment of my life, I don't feel like I need Jesus – sorry, Aunty Kath, the yellow bible has sat on my bookshelf since I saw you. And even if I did, I'm not sure I could make that leap of faith that Maddy, Sabrina and Kath have made: to completely separate their love for Christ from the church's wrongdoing. For me, the noise of its shortcomings is too loud to hear the voice of God, the Father Almighty, anymore – even if he's out there. But surely something is out there, I ask when I turn to my boyfriend in bed, our heads leaning together under our yellow bedlight. We both agree there is a place we go when we die, because thinking anything else is too scary. But here on earth?

Many years ago, I was employed to look after the choristers at King's College Catholic boarding school in Cambridge: perhaps the most famous Catholic – indeed Christian – choir on earth. Each week, the Sunday choir practice was held in the gigantic chapel of Kings, one of the finest examples of late perpendicular Gothic English architecture anywhere. Its floors were one giant marble chessboard, and the walls had four arched windows that ran almost the entire length. The glass, stained by what looked like coral – glowing reds, intense greens, bright aquas and buttery yellows all swirled in ocean blue. There was the biggest brass organ I'd ever seen in my life. Everything was held together by curved stone, bending into walls that reached up into a multi-layered ceiling. To this day, I am dumbfounded that I was a frequent visitor to such a historical and significant piece of Catholicism, without really believing in it. A trespasser at heart. Yet it was that side of the faith – the grand strokes and gestures of architecture, the echoes of hundreds of attendees and choristers singing in unison, the luminance of dozens of candles all lit in a row – that moved me. It's pretty unbelievable, standing in such a church, trying to convince yourself that a father, a son and a holy spirit are the cause of it all. But the memory of that place still gives me goosebumps now.

What Happened to Safa Annour?

Introduction by
Michael Brissenden

I have to say when I first met Dan to discuss his project, I thought, 'Wow, this is going to be hard.' He told me the story – or what he knew of it – of the little Sudanese girl who was murdered in a quiet Canberra suburb and forgotten. Who was she? Who killed her? Why did it seem like no one cared? What happened to the case? Where was the mother? The news of the death came and went. The police gave a desultory mention of it in a press conference months after the little girl had died and then the whole thing went cold. The story had touched a nerve in Dan; as he says, it 'haunted' him and he wanted to know more.

And so, the investigation began.

The outcome, this remarkable piece, is the result of dogged determination, what we might once have called great 'shoe leather' journalism and a little bit of luck that only comes from giving something the time it deserves.

Dan went door to door around where Safa lived, talking to anyone he could find; he burrowed into the factionalised world of the Sudanese immigrant community; he uncovered the family's traumatic refugee story; his inquiries led him to imams and cultural groups; he tracked people who might have information about the little girl and her mother on social media, and he eventually found people who, while still unwilling to go public, were prepared to fill in some of the background, to put some substance around little Safa's life.

The police were still refusing to discuss the case at all, believing that this pesky reporter probably didn't have much information anyway and, well aware that the media has an ever-shortening attention span, assuming he would soon lose interest.

Dan kept at them, presented them with everything he'd discovered, including the relationship Safa's mother was in at the time, with an older male refugee who suffered from PTSD. Shortly after the little girl's death, it is believed that man returned to Sudan.

But, despite it all, the police remained an impenetrable wall. Perhaps because to acknowledge what they knew would be also to acknowledge their failure. Four years after Safa died, the mostly white ACT police force still couldn't solve this crime – perhaps because they simply couldn't find the bridge into a suspicious and wary immigrant community.

The system, it seems, had already made up its mind. Shortly after the little girl's death, her mother lost access to her other child when child protection authorities removed Safa's brother into care.

This is not just the sad story of the death of a little girl. It is also a sad reflection of us.

Why does the death of some children resonate so deeply with the public, while the death of others – often black or Indigenous – does not generate the frenzied media interest and demands for justice?

The crime may never be solved, but at least this story will ensure Safa will not be another forgotten death.

What Happened to Safa Annour?

Dan Jervis-Bardy

PORTION II OF GUNGAHLIN CEMETERY WAS IN A PARTICULARLY
unkempt state on this overcast and unseasonably muggy morning
in late October 2022. Rain from a third consecutive La Niña had
left Canberra overgrown. Grass was creeping up against the head-
stones and weeds were starting to overwhelm the lawns. It had the
appearance of a place that didn't get much love.

I was there to find a grave marked with a small white tag and a
misspelt name.

Along the row reserved for children, I spotted a handful of these
tags attached to the cobblestone plots. Some were clean, the names
of the deceased easy to identify; others were harder due to the dirt
or mould that had somehow breached the laminated cover.

But none was hers.

What marked her plot was no longer a generic white tag but
a purple plaque with gold lettering. It featured the silhouette of a
butterfly, bursting into the sky. I couldn't read the Arabic writing,
but the date of death confirmed it was hers.

More than four and a half years had passed since Safa Abubakr Annour was buried here after what police believed was her murder. All that time had passed with no arrests or answers, justice or closure, or even a sign that someone cared.

This purple plaque was not grand, but it told me – for the first time – that someone did.

Safa Annour was happy and healthy.

At least that's how it appeared as she was led off the bus holding the hand of a woman dressed in a golden headscarf, who was clasping a children's backpack branded with characters from *Finding Nemo*. Safa waved enthusiastically to the driver as she walked past, and again before she was helped onto the footpath on Stuart Street.

The street cuts through Griffith, an old and prestigious part of Canberra's inner-south known for its wide verges, mature trees and large painted-brick homes with pitched terracotta roofs. It also has its share of public housing, pockets of disadvantage not far from the halls of power inside Parliament House.

Another child had rushed off the bus and onto the footpath, appearing impatient as they waited for Safa and the woman to catch up.

It was 8.40 on the morning of 30 April 2018.

The end of April marks the slow descent into winter in Canberra. Anzac Day is regarded by locals as the first time it is acceptable to turn on the household heater.

Safa was wearing a dark-green overcoat that morning, which covered most of her small torso. Her hair was bunched in yellow ties, the same type she was wearing in the only picture police released of her.

She was dead that afternoon, unable to be resuscitated after being taken to Canberra Hospital at about 1.50 pm. An autopsy would conclude she had died of internal bleeding from blunt force trauma.

Police believed she was murdered, nineteen days short of her third birthday. What happened to Safa Annour?

Almost nothing is known about her life, let alone what transpired in the hours after she stepped off the bus that morning. The police, who waited six months to tell the public about her death, had made no arrests or named suspects. There had been no coronial inquest, nor public pressure for one. No relatives came forward with public tributes or demands for answers, nor did members of Canberra's small Sudanese community, to which Safa briefly belonged. There were no candlelight vigils, no #Justice4Safa hashtags on social media or GoFundMe pages – the symbols of mourning in the modern age.

The police and ACT government blanketed the case with a thick veil of secrecy, refusing to answer the media's most basic questions or confirm the most basic facts, including that the woman on the bus was Safa's mother and the other child her older brother.

What was left was silence.

It was the mystery that hooked me.

It was the silence that haunted me.

How can it be that a toddler is seen on a public bus in the morning, is dead that afternoon in a suspected murder and, years on, authorities cannot or will not say what happened, let alone bring a perpetrator to justice?

And what does it say about Canberra, the nation's most socially progressive, affluent and educated population, that a little black child was murdered in one of its neighbourhoods and then all but forgotten?

These two questions occupied a permanent space in my mind for much of the previous four years, gripping me in a way the hundreds of other stories I covered in that period never did.

The names and faces of children murdered, lost, taken or abused are seared into our consciousness: Azaria Chamberlain, William Tyrrell, Cleo Smith.

But nobody talks about Safa Annour.

This is a story about the mysterious death of a toddler in the national capital.

It is also a story about silence: the things that create it and the things that sustain it.

I was working the breaking news shift for the *Canberra Times* when ACT Policing called a press conference at its Belconnen headquarters on the morning of 1 November 2018.

The police beat is often dull in Canberra. The sorts of major crimes that keep journalists busy in places like Sydney and Melbourne – murders, gang violence, drug busts – are rare in the nation's capital.

The reporters and camera crew crammed inside Winchester police station's media room that morning were unaware of exactly what was to be announced when Detective Superintendent Scott Moller approached the lectern.

Moller would reveal, for the first time publicly, that a two-year-old named Safa Annour had died on 30 April in what police suspected was a murder.

Strongly built, bald and with piercing ice-blue eyes, the veteran detective spoke in slow, deliberate sentences, his tone unchanged by the subject he described. Safa's death, he said plainly, was 'absolutely horrendous'.

Police circulated the CCTV footage retrieved from the bus, which captured Safa waving to the driver on the morning of the day she died. They also published a photograph of the toddler sitting alone on a stone step. Her yellow top matched the ties in her hair. She was wearing a white jumper, blue jeans and silver sneakers with velcro straps. A row of plain silver bangles hung around her left wrist. Her brown eyes stared into the eye of the camera, her expression neither a frown nor a smile. She looked older than two.

Moller shared the facts police were prepared to share and nothing more: the bus trip, the exact time she was taken to Canberra Hospital, the autopsy's finding and the belief that she was the victim of a horrible crime.

Police had established that two people were responsible for Safa's care at the time she suffered the fatal injuries, but refused to name them, disclose what relationship they had to her or confirm if they were persons of interests or suspects in the case.

They wouldn't confirm the identities of the woman and other child on the bus, whose faces were blurred in the CCTV footage. Moller said police had been 'vigorously' investigating numerous lines of inquiry but wouldn't say what they were.

Police believed there were people in Canberra with information about Safa's suspected murder who hadn't yet come forward. This was an appeal to them.

ACT Policing, a branch of the Australian Federal Police that
the ACT government contracts to service the territory, had a habit
of revealing details of cases or appealing for public assistance only
as a last resort and often months after the event.

As for the six-month delay in informing the public of Safa's
suspected murder, Moller offered only this:

> At the time of her death, we made a decision not to release those
> details to the public. Since that time, the investigation has taken us
> along a line of inquiry and we have decided to release these details.

The toddler's death received extensive media coverage that day,
prompting an outpouring of grief on social media. But after police
refused requests for further detail and no family members, friends,
community leaders or neighbours came forward to shed light on
her short life or tragic death, there was no immediate follow-up.

There would be another burst of coverage a fortnight later
when police released a second clip of CCTV footage, this time
from the day before Safa's death, in another appeal for the public's
help.

Around 9.40 am on Sunday, 29 April, a home security camera
caught Safa, her brother and a woman walking south on Sturt
Avenue, Narrabundah – the suburb immediately east of Griffith.
Police wanted to speak with the woman, who was white and dressed
in office attire, but stressed that she wasn't a suspect. That night
television news packages quoted anonymous neighbours hoping for
justice for the dead child.

After that, just three stories were published about the unsolved
murder over the next eight months. The final one, published on

1 June 2019, was the most revealing. Two old colleagues at the *Canberra Times*, who had spent months investigating the case, reported that Safa, her mother and brother had been receiving 'crisis support' and living away from home at the time of the toddler's death. The article raised the question of whether a suspect might have fled overseas.

The police refused to confirm or deny any of it. The reason for the secrecy was never explained.

The forces that propel a news story slowed, then stopped, causing the tragedy to recede and then disappear from the public's attention.

The first, second, third and fourth anniversaries of Safa's death passed without mention in the media or further police appeals for information. The reporters who followed the case moved to different roles, as did I. The rest of the local media appeared to lose interest.

I never stopped thinking about what happened to Safa Annour.

I couldn't bear the silence.

By the time I started investigating Safa's death for this piece, in October 2022, I had reconciled myself with the possibility that no matter how hard I tried, I might not be able to uncover what happened to her. I found comfort in the prospect of a story chronicling the insurmountable barriers that prevented the truth coming out. It would be an important piece of public interest journalism that asked uncomfortable questions of police. It would ask Canberrans to confront their silence.

But I needed the assurance of one thing.

I refused to accept, even with the persisting silence, that there wasn't someone who knew and cared about Safa, who cherished her life and was grieving her death. I felt sure those people existed after visiting Portion 11 – the Islamic section – of Gungahlin Cemetery in Canberra's northern suburbs.

One of the colleagues who pursued the case visited the cemetery roughly a year after Safa died. Back then her grave was marked only with a generic ACT Cemeteries Authority tag, which had spelt her name 'Safia'. Three and a half years on, I found the purple plaque with three lines of text written in Arabic. The text was verses from the Koran about the soul returning to God after death, which is commonly used on plaques for Muslim graves.

I returned to the car to scribble a note in the diary that I was keeping during the investigation.

Someone cared for Safa.

A name, age, basic facts about Safa's last movements, her religion and the unconfirmed details from the *Canberra Times* report in June 2019. One photo and two short clips of CCTV footage. That was all I had.

Safa's background was unclear at that stage – there were only rumours that she was South Sudanese – so I started with the Islamic community. I contacted people linked with Canberra's mosques, including imams, the faith leaders whose roles include leading the Salat Al-Janazah, the traditional prayers at a Muslim funeral. None recalled Safa or her funeral.

I was at least able to establish her background was Sudanese, not South Sudanese. The two are separate countries, a fact often confused or ignored in media reporting in Australia. The former Sudan split in 2011, when the majority Christian south voted to secede after decades of marginalisation under the ruling government from the Arab–Muslim north. Conflict, drought and famine had by then forced millions of Sudanese people into refugee camps in neighbouring African countries. Thousands would settle in Australia, mostly in Victoria and New South Wales.

Canberra's Sudanese community is small, numbering just 370 people from 170 families, according to the 2021 census. It is also disconnected.

As I quickly discovered, the Sudanese had none of the organised groups, clubs or associations that are the cornerstones of other migrant communities in Canberra. I could find no community leaders, the types of people whom the media would contact after tragedies such as this.

I approached a newly formed group set up to represent African migrant communities with 'one voice' in Canberra, hoping it might have some answers. It didn't.

Nobody, it seemed, did.

I spoke to Detective Superintendent Scott Moller for the first time in late November.

The briefing was arranged on the proviso that it was off-the-record, meaning none of what was discussed during our telephone conversation could be reported.

I knew very little about the case beyond what was already known, and police weren't about to volunteer anything further. The police media team did provide an on-the-record statement a few weeks later, which confirmed the murder investigation was still active and that 'numerous lines of inquiry' were under review. But they provided no detail about those lines of inquiry and wouldn't respond directly to the series of questions I put to them, including whether a suspect had fled overseas.

My story based on the statement was published online and on page six of the *Canberra Times* on 9 January – the first media reporting about Safa in 1317 days.

I hoped the article might spur someone to come forward.

None did.

It was luck, persistence and perhaps fate that led me to people who knew Safa.

You won't find their names printed here. Their requests for privacy, just like their silence until now, shouldn't be misinterpreted: people cared about her.

They attended her burial on 10 May 2018. They wanted answers, justice and closure.

The breakthroughs started in the first weeks of January after three months trawling the internet, in particular social media, searching for clues. Each piece of information I gathered – starting with the names of family members – helped illuminate what had once been hidden.

I learned where Safa had come from, where she was living at the time of her death and the traumatic chain of events that unfolded after it. The more I learned, the more tragic the story became. The more I uncovered, the more I understood why there was silence.

*

Darfur is a vast and mostly desolate region of western Sudan. It is known internationally for the bloody violence that erupted in 2003 after rebel groups launched an insurrection against the Arab-dominated government. Then-president Omar al-Bashir responded by arming militia groups – known as the Janjaweed – who carried out mass killings of Darfuri men, women and children. The United Nations in 2013 estimated that up to 300,000 people had been killed and 3 million displaced in what has been referred to as the first genocide of the twenty-first century.

Safa Annour arrived in Australia in July 2017 with her older brother, father Abubakr and mother Huda, as refugees from this troubled part of East Africa. It is believed the family escaped to Indonesia before reaching Canberra.

There's a photo of the four of them together in what appears to be a department store, Safa in her mother's arms. She couldn't have been much older than eighteen months. Abubakr, wearing a Bintang Beer top under a black jacket, is resting his arms over his son's shoulders.

Word of the young family's arrival in Canberra spread among members of the local Sudanese community, who helped them settle in. They had once been in their shoes: new in a foreign land, far from family, unfamiliar with the language and culture and offered very little help from the government.

Safa was said to be a smiling, bubbly child. The enthusiastic waves to the bus driver on the morning of 30 April 2018 – that was Safa.

I found a third photo of her, this time with her brother, sitting on the edge of a fountain. She had bright-pink ties in her hair, matching the colour of her shirt and boots. The same row of silver bangles hung loosely around the left wrist. She wasn't staring straight at the camera. This time her head was turned, eyes glancing back, the first hint of a cheeky grin emerging at the corner of her mouth.

In the months after arriving in Canberra, her parents' relationship is understood to have frayed. Abubakr relocated interstate and Safa, her mother and brother moved into a home for women, not far from the bus stop on Stuart Street. That was where the toddler was living in the days before she died.

Police descended on the home after Safa's death and spent hours poring over security camera footage from nearby properties.

I won't disclose the location of the home, and I was careful to avoid it when I doorknocked the street, hoping to find neighbours who might recall what happened four and a half years earlier.

I was about to leave after a fruitless forty-five minutes when a burly man with tattoos up and down his arms approached the car, motioned for me to wind down the window and asked what I was doing.

I replied that I was a reporter investigating the suspected murder of a toddler and showed him a picture of Safa.

He didn't need reminding.

He said he was away at the time, but his partner was here and had vivid recollections of a commotion at the home in the days before 30 April 2018. His partner had suspicions about what happened, he said, but it was best I hear them from her directly.

She never returned my calls or text messages.

*

Among the few details police revealed at that first press conference was that two unnamed people were responsible for Safa's care when she suffered her fatal injuries.

Her mother, Huda, I was able to establish, was one of them. The other person was a Sudanese man Huda had befriended in Canberra named Luay Shaor. Both were present at the hospital on the night Safa died, along with other members of the Sudanese community and police.

At that early stage the toddler's death wasn't being treated as a possible murder. But when the results of the post-mortem came in, police ramped up their investigation.

Huda's daughter had not yet been buried when child protection stepped in and took her son.

The intervention was detailed in an email the mother sent months later to the ACT Human Rights Commission in a desperate plea for its help so she could see her son face to face. Huda told the commission that the Child and Youth Protection Service (CYPS) had removed her son four days after Safa's death because it was being treated as 'suspicious'. She felt authorities had made up their minds that she was involved. She wrote that CYPS had banned her from supervised visits to her son, restricting their interactions to video calls.

She was a grieving mother, practically alone in a foreign country, battling a system she didn't understand. She wanted to see her son and for him to see her, so that he would know his mother hadn't abandoned him.

CYPS is permitted under ACT law to remove a child from the care of their parent for forty-eight hours if it believes the child must live somewhere else to be safe. The agency must then apply to the children's court to retain parental responsibility beyond those first two days.

For legal reasons, the ACT government would not confirm if it launched the emergency intervention, let alone if any action was taken on the grounds Huda was involved in Safa's death. It would not confirm whether or not Safa was known to authorities before she died.

The minister responsible for the ACT's child protection system, Rachel Stephen-Smith, confirmed she was briefed on the case because of the 'unusual circumstances' of the toddler's death. Stephen-Smith was given a summary of what was known about Safa's life up to then, according to a brief statement her office provided to me.

The briefing was on 4 May 2018, one day after CYPS stepped in and took Safa's brother, according to the timeline set out in the mother's email to the Human Rights Commission.

I tried to contact Huda.

She didn't respond.

Luay Shaor came to Australia with his brother in 2001 with the help of the United Nations High Commissioner for Refugees. The siblings were initially based in Tasmania before Luay left for Sydney, where he started a construction business.

The facts were detailed in court documents for a civil case that Luay's brother and his partner had launched against Canberra Hospital.

Luay was holding down a full-time job and had a family when, in 2013, he was sentenced to three months' weekend detention for bashing a man in his sixties. Court documents show Luay reacted to the older man hurling abuse and throwing stones by beating him, leaving him with fractures to both eye sockets, nasal bone and left ring finger.

The court heard Luay suffered from chronic post-traumatic stress disorder, which developed after an 'extraordinarily difficult upbringing' in Sudan.

The magistrate accepted there was a connection between his condition and the bashing, but found it didn't in and of itself explain it.

Luay had no criminal record and was praised for his work in the Sudanese community, according to the *Canberra Times* report from his sentencing hearing. His Facebook page painted an image of a doting single father whose life purpose was his daughter.

I tried to contact Luay.

He didn't respond.

I couldn't establish when Luay befriended Huda or the exact nature of their relationship. But multiple sources with knowledge of the case confirmed he spent time with the children, including on the day Safa died.

Huda took a driving lesson that day, during which time she was away from the children.

She remained in Canberra as she dealt with the fallout of her daughter's death and son's removal.

Luay didn't.

It is believed he left Australia and returned to Sudan in the months after 30 April 2018.

*

I never spoke to Scott Moller again.

It was not for a lack of trying. For weeks I pestered the police media team to arrange a meeting – even off-the-record – so I could put to them the long list of questions I now had.

Eventually, I was told he would be unavailable.

Around the same time, I was also trying to contact the ACT coroner to understand why an inquest hadn't been held. The coroner's office wouldn't grant a briefing and wouldn't speculate on a possible future inquiry, noting that a criminal investigation was underway.

Sources close to the case pointed to another factor, however. The ACT only appointed its first dedicated coroner in February 2022. Magistrates had until then been 'on-call' to oversee inquests, leading to a backlog of cases that prolonged the wait for answers for bereaved families.

Some of the families formed advocacy groups to lobby politicians and appeared in the media holding framed photos of their loved ones.

No one came forward with framed photos of Safa Annour.

The police eventually arranged a briefing with another senior officer, Detective Sergeant Matt Innes, for midday on 9 March. We spoke for just under an hour in a sterile conference room in ACT Policing's city station, and I told him everything I knew.

This briefing was also off the record. But we had agreed that the police would provide a written statement that could be used in this piece.

The silence was going to be broken.

*

The basic facts about Safa's life, including who was responsible for her care when she sustained the fatal injuries, were not disputed. But police would not confirm, or deny, anything of substance about the investigation. They would not disclose who had been interviewed, arguing that doing so could jeopardise the investigation.

They would not be drawn on whether Luay was still in Australia, although they confirmed that, as a general rule, authorities did not have the power to stop someone who hadn't been charged with a crime from leaving the country. Australia does not have an extradition treaty with Sudan, meaning that even if charges were laid there was no guarantee its government would assist with deportation.

I had learned one of the reasons the case had been hidden from the public for six months was that it was treated as a domestic incident.

Innes wouldn't confirm that either, saying only that the police's 'investigative strategy determined no immediate public messaging was required'.

I hoped there might be some answers in the internal police records produced during the six-month period, which I applied to access using freedom of information laws. A tranche of 120 such documents existed, including case notes and emails, but the police's lawyers refused to let me see them, arguing that their release could reveal lines of inquiry and prejudice the investigation.

There were some things Innes would confirm. One of them deepened the mystery.

Safa's demeanour on the bus on the morning of 30 April 2018 led to the assumption that she suffered her fatal injuries in the five-hour period before she was taken to hospital.

But Innes revealed that police had not ruled out the possibility that rather than one fatal blow, Safa died from an accumulation of blunt force traumas inflicted on her in the days prior.

But that wasn't the main reason the investigation had so far come to nothing.

Sudanese people tend to be wary of police.

Their experience in Sudan taught them that uniformed men in authority could harm them – even torture and kill them – rather than help them. To understand the silence, I had to understand this, according to Sudanese Australians who spoke to me for this piece.

Detectives assigned to Safa's case had trouble encouraging members of the Sudanese community to come forward and extracting information from them.

After they made the first public appeal, on 1 November 2018, police were not inundated with information. ACT Policing, which has little cultural diversity in its ranks, turned to specialist branches of the federal police for help to navigate the cultural barriers.

Innes said dealing with the cultural practices and conventions of the Sudanese community proved 'challenging', but not insurmountable.

I learned that the distrust of authority was combined with a culture of privacy. The idea of approaching the media to air a personal, private matter – as those families who pushed for coronial inquests did – is foreign to Sudanese people. One of the reasons is to avoid bringing negative attention, including shame, to one's family and community. Speaking up wasn't something that was done.

'Most newly arrived Sudanese don't feel they can have a voice, or that anyone would support them if they raise their voice,' one Sudanese Australian migrant told me. 'People choose to be silent.'

Without naming individuals, Innes confirmed that people with information about Safa's death had chosen to remain silent. But as the five-year anniversary approached, he insisted police remained committed to the case. 'The death of any child is a tragedy – more so when it is believed to be the result of another person's actions,' he said.

What happened to Safa Annour?

I can't answer that question.

Perhaps the coroner is now the only person who can.

I can, however, try to explain the silence.

It started with ACT Policing and its disposition for secrecy, a mentality shared by the territory government.

It was sustained because, aside from those two reporters in the first eight months, the local media chose not to dedicate its ever-thinning resources to the case.

The media's interest in tragedies like these so often relies on the families who speak up, who pose for photos with framed images of their loved ones. As the years passed and nobody from Safa's marginalised migrant community spoke up to demand justice, neither did we.

Perhaps that is why this case haunted me.

I was complicit.

We cannot know what might have come from persistent pressure that was never applied, or outrage that never erupted. We cannot know the cost of our silence.

But imagine for a moment if her name was Sarah, not Safa.

Imagine that her hair was blonde, not brown, and that her skin was white, not black.

Don't tell me it wouldn't have been different.

Broken Chains

How Australia's food supply network is fatally flawed

Introduction by Margaret Simons

One of the first things I said to Esther Linder was that there was no substitute, in writing narrative non-fiction, for going places. In a story about Australia's food supply chains, there are so many possible starts to the story. Esther already had good contacts in the academic community, for example. She had written on aspects of the food supply chain story before. She had facts, quotes and opinions at her fingertips. But, for my money, her work came alive when she went to Forbes, New South Wales – the heart of the industrial-scale farming country that lies behind those supply chains.

Having been there, seen people, watched as cattle were bought and sold and loaded onto trucks, Esther's next step was the one that so many writers find difficult – privileging your own perceptions and understandings, and using them to bring the story alive. Writers – all writers, but perhaps particularly those who are close to the beginning of their career – often struggle with the questions 'Why me?' 'What right do I have to impose my understandings on the reader?'

I have a response I have used with dozens of students. I am sure Esther got tired of hearing it. You can't dodge the role of the narrator. Who is telling the story to whom and under which circumstances? There can only be one answer in non-fiction. Whether you like it or not, whether you feel qualified or not, the narrator is you. The role of the narrator is fundamental to human storytelling – archetypal, in fact. And storytelling is one of the things that make us human.

The narrative intelligence is always there, even if it is not explicit. It is the writer who gathers and collates the facts, and chooses how to display them, pointing out to the reader what there is to learn from these events and settings, and how they connect to their own experiences.

The first paragraph of this piece, describing the trucks that carry Australia, that keep us fed, came late in the process. For me, that paragraph lands us in the middle of the story, connecting the narrative Esther tells to an experience that most of us have had, driving on this continent.

That paragraph is the mark of the narrator. It is a heroic role, and the sign of a true writer.

Broken Chains

Esther Linder

MOVING INTO THE TWILIGHT, HOUR UPON HOUR, KILOMETRE upon kilometre, they are inescapable. Every road and corner, every petrol stop and park. Wheels grind over tarred roads, trailer loads shake with the speed. They are backbone and skin, flesh negotiable. I drove into the night, travelling deeper into New South Wales and the country that feeds us. The other cars faded. The trucks were my companions. They are always there, always moving. If Australia were to be picked up and carried elsewhere, it would be on the back of a B-double prime mover.

When I passed them, I became short of breath. The noise stopped for a millisecond, and I tried to curl myself into a tighter ball to make myself smaller, the psychological threat of the truck's onslaught looming larger than the knowledge of already being inside my own vehicle. A squeeze, a flash, and sound returned. Roaring on, the road train continued. Getting food from one place to another, a farmyard or distribution centre or port its next destination. Our diet, the contents of what we carry from plate to mouth, is carried upon the back of such machines.

The breadth and complexity of the trade routes across the continent make it incredible that one thing does indeed get some-place else – to your doorstep in a grocery bag, specially packed and delivered, containing items brought from all corners of the continent and globe.

This essay is not about the chain of events taken to get an apple to the fruit bowl on the kitchen table. Rather, it is a story about all the things that could go wrong so that the fruitbowl remains empty. It is a story about how broken links, a hodgepodge of policy, and an incomplete idea of what it means for the climate to be irrevocably changing make us vulnerable. The things we take for granted may soon no longer exist.

All roads lead to Rome, they said. In rural Australia, in the landscapes that make up our food-growing regions, all roads lead to a supermarket.

Australia's grocery sector is dominated by two major players: Coles Supermarkets Australia and the Woolworths Group, together forming around 65 per cent of the market. Aldi makes up around 11 per cent, with that share growing year on year, and independent grocers and supermarkets fill in the gaps. In a sector with an overbearing push for profits, a lack of competition and increasing impact by climate change, these main players have an oversized impact on the way we eat.

Where they coalesce and break apart is the distribution centre – an aortic valve in the network, invisible to most. In the industrial

estates in Melbourne's outer ring, warehouses and truck saleyards
sit side by side along roads that are wide enough to accommodate
road trains. Three turns off the Western Ring Road in Truganina,
a distribution centre is ringed by security fencing, a gigantic metal
box lit by fluorescent lighting day and night. Loading bays open
out into the world like the many maws of an inanimate beast,
spewing forth everything a functioning supermarket requires.
Across the entrance is emblazoned 'Coles Laverton CDC' in big
red-and-white lettering.

Trucks arrive and depart at all hours of the day and night. It is
a 24/7 operation that tends to the constant demand of consumers
to be supplied with everything, everywhere, all at once. Inside,
forklifts move between the loading bays and the endless aisles
of pallets, shifting things one step closer to a supermarket shelf.
This single distribution centre supplies chilled refrigerated goods
such as milk, eggs and dairy to Coles outlets across Victoria and
Tasmania. The interior stays at the temperature of a fridge.

'I never realised how big it was to get our food to us, but
it's huge,' an employee said to me – *it* being the complexity of
the distributional network. Suppliers deliver their goods here
via truck, which are then processed and placed on one of the
hundreds of Coles-emblazoned trucks that move through this
centre every day. On the darker roads around the centre, trailers
sit semi-abandoned as prime movers are switched out. I drive past
rest stops, truck drivers asleep in their cabs next to lone eucalyptus
trees. Underneath a characteristically dreary Melbourne sky, rain
sweeps through in waves. The roads are slick with it.

*

In early March 2023, there were reports that a refrigerated transportation company specialising in chilled foods was going to go under. Scott's Refrigerated Logistics was the sole transporter of cold goods for Coles and Aldi, and a major supplier to the rest of the grocery industry since the 1960s. Lamb chops for a weeknight dinner, milk and eggs, frozen peas: all trucked in and out of about twenty-four of the company's distribution centres around the country and sent to your local supermarket to be swiftly unpacked and placed on a freezer or fridge shelf. After the company was placed into voluntary administration in February 2023, administrators KordaMentha, as reported by the *Australian Financial Review* in April[1], managed to recoup $100 million in asset sales of the 1800-odd trucks and trailers that were the physical remnants of the business. Leases for company sites were wound up, people laid off and a full stop placed on the ledger books.

During the chaos of the company's collapse, half a billion dollars' worth of frozen food had lain unclaimed in the company's cold storage warehouses for several weeks. Fifteen hundred people were left jobless and five hundred prime mover trucks taken off the road. The federal minister for transport, Catherine King, noted the liquidation 'with disappointment', as headlines proliferated about whether Australia could manage this new crisis of supply. 'We urge those parties who remain involved in the liquidation to work together quickly to reach an agreement that keeps trucks on the road and food on the shelves,' she said in a joint statement with the minister for employment, Tony Burke.

The major supermarkets responded with icy resolve. Coles said that they were no longer dependent on the company and had

---

1 Thompson, Sarah, Sood, Kanika and Rapaport, Emma, 'KordaMentha Hauls in $100m from Sale of Scott's Refrigerated Trucks', *Australian Financial Review*, 18 April 2023.

engaged other options. Others echoed the corporate speak but gave no details as to how they would cope with a key thread of the distributional chain destroyed. The Transport Workers Union predicted more collapses because of 'a race to the bottom' between trucking companies to fulfil the demands of increasingly tight budgets, inflation overall, and corporate clients demanding the lowest possible costs.

Storing and transporting food that needs to be kept cold or frozen is complicated. It requires refrigeration at every step of the journey, staff trained in complex equipment, and a market that can pay for all that. Rising energy costs are making refrigeration more expensive, and clients are demanding cheaper alternatives. Scott's Refrigerated Logistics is not the first trucking company to fail in an industry plagued by a labour shortage, spiking fuel costs and clients hellbent on cutting costs.

Neither Coles nor Woolworths responded to detailed requests for comment for this story, but their media departments forwarded their latest financial statements by way of making sense of business. Overwhelmingly, the statements show that the focus on natural disasters and issues within the supply chain do not correlate with smaller profits for either supermarket. Instead, both recorded double-digit profit rises, a dynamic that is directly noted in a report by the Australia Institute in February: 'Supermarket profits have soared on the strength of rapid food price inflation.' Coles made $1.098 billion in net profits (after tax) for the full 2023 financial year, a 4.8 per cent increase on the year prior.[2] Woolworths made a staggering $1.618 billion.[3]

2   2023 Full year results release, Coles Group Limited, 22 August 2023.
3   Woolworths Group Annual Report 2023, 23 August 2023.

At the same time, Coles' half-yearly report notes 'increasing cost pressures' for the company as well as the impacts of natural disasters such as the sole railway supplying Perth, the Trans-Australian, being devastated by flooding. At the time of Woolworths releasing their results in late February, the company's CEO Brad Banducci outlined how food sales had increased 6.5 per cent since the beginning of the year.[4] Banducci linked this rise to the cost-of-living crisis, as people were choosing to eat at home rather than spending more money eating out.

Inflation continues to rise, but the extent to which corporate profits are outstripping CPI increases is ungodly. Dr Jim Stanford, the author of 'Profit-Price Spiral: The Truth Behind Australia's Inflation', published by the Australia Institute[5], directly links the profit-taking to a profit-cost loop, saying, 'Without the inclusion of those excess profits in final prices for Australian-made goods and services, inflation since the pandemic would have been much slower.' At the same time, real wages are falling, natural disasters are becoming a monthly occurrence and our food chains are stretching. The price hikes instigated by supermarkets such as Coles and Woolworths, ascribed as a necessary evil given the problems in the supply chain and rising costs elsewhere, are in fact contributing to a spiral that cannot be easily rectified.

To understand where this story begins and could end will take time. What happened with Scott's, the vulnerabilities implied by having two states supplied with staples from a single distribution

4   Kaye, Byron and Manekar, Sameer, 'Australian Grocer Woolworths Says Inflation Is Spurring In-home Dining', Reuters, 22 February 2023.
5   Stanford, J, 'Profit-Price Spiral: The Truth Behind Australia's Inflation', The Australia Institute: Centre for Future Work, 23 February 2023.

node, and the endpoint of ever-increasing supermarket prices work together like pieces of a Jenga tower. Move one piece, and the whole food chain might fall.

At the bottom of this tower is the earth, and what comes from it. In Australia, the Murray–Darling Basin is the continent's food bowl. Three states, 2.3 million people, five parliaments, 77,000 kilometres of river, and 7300 farms are made possible by the water that flows through the basin. The millions of tonnes of grains, fruit, vegetables and more produced here are loaded onto trucks and sent to processing plants, factories or distribution centres to be exported overseas or sold around the country. But the costs of production are increasing, the food is increasingly expensive, and the vulnerabilities of the supply chain have become increasingly apparent.

Two hours' drive north of the New South Wales–Victoria border, the roads trace endless hazy golden-brown fields of cereal croppage. This is Wiradjuri Country, where the sky and land expands into a never-ending vista of stubbly earth. During December and January each year, the land is shorn of its crops of wheat, oats and barley. Combine harvesters chop each stalk into its requisite parts, which are loaded, sorted, processed and loaded again. Some of the trillions of individual grains are put into farm silos, saved for the meagre seasons and the droughts. Most are loaded onto trucks, then onto trains and finally ships. From there, a Jackson Pollock web of international shipping routes takes European grains grown on Aboriginal lands and carries them into the global economy.

Back on Wiradjuri Country, the Riverina region of the Basin, the fields are picked over by livestock or burned off before being rested and sown again. More calories grown, watered and harvested, and then more journeys.

After harvest, the land is the gold-tipped brown that suggests dust. Only a few years ago, in 2019, these fields were bone-dry, roots cracking and aquifers empty. Livestock were given feed trucked in from elsewhere, and not all of them survived. The memory of this time lies just under the surface. Such times will come again. The Millennium Drought – between the end of the previous century and 2009 – is said to have been the worst drought in colonial memory. It ended with catastrophic floods beginning in 2020 that boded the end of the drought and the beginning of the La Niña cycle.

Growing and supplying food in Australia is dependent on the sun and the rain, the people and their machines, and the roads taken to get things from one place to another. Knock out one of these cogs and the wheels fall off.

In Forbes, in central New South Wales, the rains started in August 2022 and kept bucketing down. Everything turned into mud and churn, and in November, the waters peaked and the town flooded. Five months later, there are still circular pieces missing from the tar, as though someone has taken a giant ice-cream scoop to them.

The mayor of Forbes, Phyllis Miller, is blunt in her assessment of the damage and its cost: 'Horrendous.' The road damage alone, in an area where everything is moved via road, will take up to two years to repair. This is partly due to a lack of tradespeople, as well as funding delays.

Unacknowledged, and largely unplanned for, are the inevitable future disasters as the climate changes. 'We don't look that far ahead, really,' she says. 'We got flooded last year and the year before. We still had not got our flood money from the November before's flood . . . So now we've got to go back and reassess all of those roads. It's just a nightmare. It's really a convoluted system, the way you get your money.'

The money Miller is referring to is a combination of federal and state disaster funding, comprising various grants, of which some are automatically released and others requiring complex applications and assessments. Forbes Shire was given $2.5 million at the time of the 2021 floods from the state government, and six road crews from Transport NSW to work on the major roads, but there is still endless work to do.

'Our best guess is that it's going to take us a couple of years to get back on top of our road network,' she tells me.

Among many of the farmers is a reluctance to even acknowledge the climate is changing any more than it always has.

Within an hour of first contacting Tom Matthews, I am meandering down the gravel driveway of his property, Montana, a sheep and cereals farm near Grenfell, in central-west New South Wales. His skin is baked from years in the sun, covered in part by a cornflower-blue short-sleeved shirt. An akubra sits on his head, sweat-stained, beginning to develop holes and partially bent at the cap. His syllables are blunt, his vowels long and his manner businesslike. He launches into an explanation of how his farm works, its history and the current economics of crutching sheep.

Crutching – the removal of wool from the rear of a sheep for hygiene purposes – has to be done before breeding season to prevent infection, and it is a specialised skill. Tom pays up to $4000 a week to two blokes who don't turn up half the time, because they know there is no one else and he has no choice but to keep hiring them. Crutching his herd of 6500 sheep cost him $22,000 prior to my visit.

Thanks to La Niña, Matthews benefited from disaster funding available to individuals and farm-holdings after the floods that hit Forbes at the end of 2022. He used it to repair fencing, build a dam and replace some of his farming equipment. But, meanwhile, the price of everything needed for the everyday running of a farm has gone up.

His main costs are freight, which has doubled, and other administrative bills. 'Insurance premiums are astronomical,' Matthews says, and because of the cost of parts, his repair and maintenance bills have doubled in the last three years.

'We're a price-taker not a price-maker, and we pay freight both ways,' he tells me matter-of-factly, and shows me a text message from GrainCorp stating the current market prices for oats, wheat and other grains: ranging between $250 per tonne for low-grade wheat to just over $600 for high-grade canola. 'So we pay freight to get our fertiliser out here, then we pay freight to get our product out to port. Last year our fertiliser cost was double what it was the year before, and we planted less crop, because it rained and we didn't get a chance to get it all in.'

Despite this, the rains have meant that crops for the past three seasons have been tremendous, and there is surplus to store on the farm to prepare for leaner seasons. But when I ask if he worries about the potential of another devastating drought, and about climate change, he demurs.

'You probably wouldn't find that many people who pay that much attention to it, in all honesty. Unfortunately, that's probably not the answer you want to hear, but that's just the reality out here. Only because you live and you breathe it, you know,' Matthews says as he gestures around to the stubby red and brown fields we are driving through. 'And we've seen it dry before, we've seen it hot before, we've seen it cold before. Look at the mild summer that we're having, it's twenty-eight degrees.'

Matthews is right – the summer is mild for that part of New South Wales. And his attitude towards climate change is common for farmers who work year-round on land that has seasonal variations. Across his farm, bees are thriving, dams are full and bumper crops have meant the silos outside the sheds where we chat are full of oats and barley.

But while it might not be apparent to him day to day, and season to season, over several lifetimes, the climate has changed irrevocably.

In April 2023, the Intergovernmental Panel on Climate Change released its most recent report on the state of global warming.[6] It described the immediate future as the 'last chance' to avert catastrophe. Among the harrowing warnings of what would happen if

6   Lee, H and Romero, J (eds.), 'IPCC Summary for Policymakers in: Climate Change 2023: Synthesis Report. Contribution of Working Groups I, II and III to the Sixth Assessment Report of the Intergovernmental Panel on Climate Change', IPCC, Geneva, Switzerland, pp. 1-34, 2023.

governments choose to continue on the path of unabated green-house gas emissions, the report's authors noted, 'It is unequivocal that human influence has warmed the atmosphere, ocean and land.' They wrote that food security, particularly in developing regions, has been greatly reduced by climate change, and 'climate-exposed sectors', such as agriculture and transport, has already suffered economic damage. The panel said it had 'high confidence' that food production would be reduced. This correlates to many other reports, some of them written in Australia, that describe how a feedback loop of increased temperatures and worsening 'natural' disasters will curb the growing of food.

Dr Arunima Malik is one of the co-authors of a study on how climate change will impact food supply chains, nutrient avail-ability, wealth and poverty in regions of Australia.[7] Her modelling showed that poorer people will be the most vulnerable to food insecurity.

'Disaster results in reductions in consumption possibilities; reduced consumption possibilities means reduced food availability outcomes for people; and then reduced food availability translates to reductions in nutrient availability,' she said. In situations where climate change has directly impacted production, such as in Forbes, the impacts are felt elsewhere too. 'If, for example, a transportation industry is reliant on transporting a certain produce from point A to point B, if the produce is not being produced, that transporta-tion route is not functional, as well, there's nothing to transport, so that transportation company is impacted,' Malik says.

---

7   Malik, A, Li, M, Lenzen, M et al, 'Impacts of Climate Change and Extreme Weather on Food Supply Chains Cascade across Sectors and Regions in Australia', *Nat Food* 3, pp. 631–643, 2022.

On the longer-term impacts of climate change, Malik has predicted 'substantial losses' at the regional level. 'The focus is not specifically on food supply chains, but the economy as a whole.' By this measure, the 'spillover impact' of crises are aggravated due to faulty links, broken chains and the ever-present risk that a product might just not be available.

And when it does eventually get to your local supermarket, the cost of the journey will be passed on. Food will simply cost more.

The Forbes Livestock Exchange sits at the heart of one of those vulnerable chains of supply. It is a soaring metal structure 12 kilometres outside the town centre, sitting like a vast spaceship that has landed on the plain. Thousands of animals move through the exchange every week, from livestock trucks into square pens, to the weighing dock, and back onto the trucks. The noises underneath the giant metal dome are amplified into a cacophony in my ears, everywhere the grassy smell of livestock and manure. The cows, sheep and pigs sold here come from as far away as southern Queensland.

Luke Whitty is one of the livestock agents who sells the animals on behalf of clients, standing atop the metal walkways of the exchange, speaking at warp speed to haggle through the hundreds of animals each day. Whitty and his colleagues bargaining and selling in tones akin to fast-paced football commentary is a theatrical performance in and of itself.

Whitty wears the light-blue shirt, blue jeans, RM Williams boots and akubra hat that are the calling cards of the region. He says that for three months during the wet weather, the roads were starting to break down and it was 'really difficult' to keep things going.

'The producers had to struggle to make that decision to sell – and where can they sell? Can they get to Forbes? Can they get to Dubbo? Can they get to Wagga? There was a little while there where the highway was shut just out of town, so a lot of people on the southern side had to go to Wagga.'

Abattoirs in Wagga Wagga, Cootamundra, Gundagai and the eastern towns towards Sydney service some of the exchange's output, but the vast majority of livestock is sold overseas. Most are slaughtered here, with the meat exported chilled or frozen, but the RSPCA estimates around 7 per cent form the remainder of the live export trade. China, our major trading partner outside of the trade wars, buys the majority of the meat. Whitty says most of the cattle that pass through Forbes would go on to China.

The data on the full cost of the last floods in Forbes won't be available for years. By then, there almost certainly will have been another flood, drought or disaster event. That is the reality of climate change. Damage to a road impacts the journey of a cow or a tonne of wheat, which bleeds into its eventual affordability or lack thereof at the supermarket.

Some hope had been placed on the $14.5 billion Inland Rail Project for food-producing regions by the then federal Coalition government. A railway link between Brisbane and Melbourne, running through the heartland of Australia's food bowl, it will span three states and connect producers and ports by train when finally completed. Current estimates are the year 2027, but budget blow-outs, timeframes and environmental concerns have already begun to concern many.

But Forbes mayor Phyllis Miller is dismissive. 'Our local knowledge is the knowledge that gets product to market,' she says, referencing the needs of individual industries across Forbes. As for the rail project, it 'hasn't come to fruition yet' and in any case it won't be fast enough for agricultural produce. Trains move too slowly and stop too often for it to be economically feasible to load refrigerated products such as meat or dairy. The implication is that whatever needs transporting must go by those vulnerable roads. If you live in a city and shop at a supermarket, chances are almost everything you're buying has been on a truck at some stage of its journey.

Road freight in Australia is estimated by Ibisworld to be worth $29.1 billion in 2023.[8] According to the National Freight Data Hub, the level of goods transported by truck is projected to grow by 77 per cent by 2050 on 2020 measures[9], as rail freight remains the main carrier for mining and minerals. The vast majority of our food is transported via highway: skeins of road, distribution centres, pallets, cold storage and milk crates, large B-double road trains and smaller two-tonne city trucks – and increasingly, food delivery services such as UberEats. What it takes to deliver something to your supermarket or directly to your door is a set of interlinked and cascading events, vehicles and hands.

And at every stage, there is cost. Associate Professor Flavio Macau is an expert in supply chains and logistics at Edith Cowan University

8   Ibisworld, 'Road Freight Transport in Australia – Market Size 2007–2028', June 2022.
9   'Navigating Australia's Freight Future', National Freight Data Hub, Department of Infrastructure, Transport, Regional Development, Communications and the Arts.

in Perth. 'Storage typically costs you money,' she says. 'And then energy prices are going up as well. So when you think about temperature control, humidity control and some other controls, you're thinking about lots of energy being used to allow that.'

Climate change introduces an extra factor – more variability. Increasingly, farmers either have a bumper crop or nothing at all. When the crop is good, there isn't enough storage capacity or the ability to move the products in a way that makes market sense. When there is nothing, the whole vast network of transport lies idle. And that idleness is itself expensive.

Macau says another vulnerability is introduced by an increasing number of large, specialist farms that have replaced many smaller family farms. In 1980, there were 120,000 cropping and dairy farms across Australia; today, there are just under 55,000 as actual production has increased year on year. The bigger farms produce one or two products – canola, wheat, oats – as opposed to the smaller and diversified landholdings once held by families. 'If this big farm is hit by an extreme weather event, it's a big impact in the supply chain,' he says. 'Some regions will suffer more than others. The more isolated you are, obviously, the more risk that extreme weather events will come and will lock you out of the market.'

Meanwhile, Australia's main supermarket companies are so reliant on single-strand chains of supply, particularly in remote areas of Australia and states such as Western Australia, that a single broken link upends the entire food network. A 2023 review of supply chain resilience by the Bureau of Infrastructure and Transport Research Economics (BITRE) found the majority of key freight routes identified as being highly vulnerable – such as the

Arnhem and Stuart Highways – were in the Northern Territory.[10] Total blockages of these supply routes from flooding are not only commonplace in the NT's wet season, but expected. 'The result is that it becomes more expensive to supply food to those places,' Macau says. The chains are fragile, and they are not subject to repair anytime soon.

A 2018 inquiry into national freight and supply chain priorities, chaired by former deputy prime minister Michael McCormack, canvassed the lack of reliable, consistent and efficient supply chains. Incredibly, food and food production were mentioned a total of three times in the entire report.[11]

In 2021, the Productivity Commission ran an inquiry into the vulnerability of Australia's supply chains.[12] It outlined how globalisation and modern business practices had resulted in a spider's web of interdependencies – factories, roads, distribution centres and farms scattered across the continent – that are fundamentally vulnerable to shocks, such as a global pandemic, a war in Ukraine and climate change. The analytical framework that the commission used considered the intersection of 'vulnerable', 'essential' and 'critical' goods and services. Food, for reasons not fully explained, was not included in the interim report and only minimally in the final.

10 Bureau of Infrastructure and Transport Research Economics, 'Road and Rail Supply Chain Resilience Review – Phase 1', February 2023 (Commonwealth of Australia).

11 Commonwealth of Australia, 'Report of the Inquiry into National Freight and Supply Chain Priorities', 2018.

12 Productivity Commission, 'Executive Summary and Findings – Vulnerable Supply Chains: Study Report', 13 August 2021.

The exclusion was described as 'peculiar' by the National Farmers' Federation (NFF) in its submission. It outlined the profound impact that even a small breakdown could have, stating that even a 'perceived breakdown' could have 'devastating impacts'.

The statements from the NFF, and those of the NSW and Victorian Farmer's Federations, had an apocalyptic tone. A breakdown of food supply chains was 'correlated' with social unrest, they said.

Though Australia has 'food sovereignty', meaning it can feed its own population without depending on imports, research done by the Climate Council of Australia suggests that by 2100, the Murray–Darling Basin will likely stop producing food for the most part because of the severity and intensity of climate-change-related weather.[13] And, on the vast wheatfields of Western Australia – which produce half of our wheat – production will have fallen by up to 49 per cent by 2090. What then?

The Office of Supply Chain Resilience, a federal branch of the Department of Industry, had no specific comment to make when asked about the vulnerabilities of food supply chains and their relationship to climate change. Instead, across the policy papers on the topic, there is a common refrain of 'building resilience' while giving a non-answer to questions about how disasters and their flow-on impacts are going to be handled.

The National Freight and Supply Chain Strategy notes that

---

13 Climate Council of Australia, 'Feeding a Hungry Nation: Climate Change, Food and Farming in Australia', 2015.

volumes of overall freight are going to increase 35 per cent by 2040, but actions include 'enable improved supply chain efficiency' as an input to implementation.[14] What does that mean? Does it mean anything at all?

There is a tendency in much political and corporate communication to obfuscate: to say nothing by saying many things. While there is much policy work that focuses on critical and longstanding issues of our time, there is also a host of issues that require attention right now.

For people such as Tom Matthews, Phyllis Miller or Luke Whitty, the direct impacts of climate change upon livelihoods and homes are already here. For those of us who do not work or live in a food-producing region, the clearest impact is at the end of the chain, when we go to buy our weekly vegetables, meat, dairy or eggs. The squeeze has already begun, with the consumer price index (CPI) increases over the last couple of years nudging 7–8 per cent. Food, one of the most non-negotiable of the non-discretionary items, is more expensive everywhere you look.

During the many hours on the road for this story, I thought about what it means when you can no longer afford food. Short- to long-term food insecurity is not a narrative Australia is familiar with, as one of the world's most prosperous countries, but it is a growing reality. In the same way that climate change cannot be ignored, how our food supply chains are fracturing also cannot be discounted. As the cost of living crisis unspools into a tsunami of need, there will be fewer avenues for politicians to avert their eyes

---

14 Commonwealth of Australia, 'Transport and Infrastructure Council: National Freight and Supply Chain Strategy', August 2019.

from the throbbing heart of the problem: more and more people cannot afford to eat properly, well or at all.

In Forbes, Orange, Cowra and some of the other places I passed through, people are recovering. Repairs are ongoing from the last floods, silos have been topped up with the most recent harvest, and livestock is moving through the markets. At the same time, the trucks roll on through the day and night, diesel fed, heavy and slow-moving. On their backs, the weight of 27 million mouths to feed and more, tensed with the possibility of another impending breakage. It won't be long.

The Best Way Out Is Always Through

Charting the course through Australia's deadlock over refugees and people seeking asylum

Introduction by
Victoria Laurie

The writer and civil rights activist James Baldwin said: 'Not everything that is faced can be changed, but nothing can be changed until it is faced.' Perhaps Hessom Razavi would only half agree with Baldwin, for his essay about Australia's refugee policy is predicated on both facing up to and changing our current stance.

Hessom is a doctor and writer whose family fled Iran in 1983 to escape political persecution. In 2015 and 2016, he visited the detention centres on Manus Island and Nauru in a medical capacity. He lives and works in Perth as an ophthalmologist, based at the Lions Eye Institute.

There's a refreshing duality to Hessom's take on everything – his perspective on the issue of Australia's refugee policy is informed by his own foreign origins and the fact that he has married into a non-refugee Australian family. There's no 'them and us', but a plea to discuss how we collectively move forward as a decent nation. Or as he puts it, 'Human lives are at stake, as is Australia's soul.'

In this essay, he dismantles the 'nuts and bolts of our policy settings' to understand our current approach to refugees, and how it could be reconfigured in a way that benefits both refugees and Australian society.

There's the tricky question about why our policies remain persistently punitive, like mandatory and indefinite detention that 'are unique by international standards and known to damage refugees'. He describes in graphic detail the self-harm and collateral injury to health due to hopelessness that he has witnessed in Australia's detention gulags.

In his medical life, Hessom has successfully led a proposal for his professional medical college to endorse, for the first time, a policy statement on the eye health of refugees and people seeking asylum. And his literary activities led to him being awarded the Behrouz Boochani Fellowship by the *Australian Book Review*.

The award was for various essays he wrote about people seeking asylum. In 'Failures of Imagination', he described his own family's flight from persecution by post-revolutionary Iran's secret police. 'The Split State' was his first attempt at systematically assessing Australia's treatment of people seeking asylum. He wrote a list and worked through it, interviewing around forty-five key figures from refugees themselves to politicians, activists and public figures. 'I was told most Aussies don't know this stuff – if they did, they might feel differently. So that's where I feel the biggest potential with refugee work is.'

He had a nagging sense that a third essay was needed – one that posits solutions and explains them in a way that makes sense to Australians other than left-leaning converts to the refugee cause. 'I want to get it in front of, and make it palatable for, a mainstream audience.'

His most convincing arguments explore real alternatives, like a Canadian scheme for community resettlement that is being modestly trialled in Australia. The Canadian scheme has resettled over 350,000 refugees since 1979, a figure that is additional to the government's normal refugee intake. It is so popular with community sponsors – who cite benefits for their town's wellbeing and economy – that a former Canadian Immigration Minister observed that he 'couldn't bring enough refugees to satisfy the Canadian demand'.

Hessom argues for 'a truly collaborative regional refugee framework with Indonesia, rather than dumping refugees illegally onto our more impoverished and less empowered neighbours'.

But he also issues a stark challenge to examine Australia's 'psychic relationship with new arrivals', our historic hostility that led to offshore and indefinite detention. One of his interviewees describes Australia as a 'melancholic torturer', with roots extending back to the dispossession of Aboriginal people.

What Hessom has done in this essay can be summed up in a quote that he furnished me with, from American poet Emily Dickinson: 'Tell all the truth but tell it slant.'

The Best Way Out Is Always Through

Hessom Razavi

I WALK IN TWO WORLDS. ONE FOOT STANDS IN AUSTRALIA'S CAMP — as a citizen, taxpayer and son-in-law to Aussies — while the other is planted with my family of origin. Forty years ago, we fled persecution in Iran to find safety here. Now, as your friends and neighbours, my message to you is simply this: Australia needs to lift its game on refugees and asylum seekers.

At a time of labour market shortages, we need the talent and entrepreneurship of refugees. In the face of historical national debt, we need the billion-dollar savings that closing offshore detention centres will deliver. Amid geopolitical tensions in the Asia–Pacific, we need diplomatic alliances with Indonesia and other neighbours, which we may encourage by sharing the responsibility for refugees with them. We need to revitalise our country towns by allowing Australians to sponsor refugees, as Canada has done for years.

There's value in enlightened self-interest. Plus, it's relevant: having receded from view, asylum seekers and refugees are back in the news.

In February 2023, Immigration Minister Andrew Giles announced that over 19,000 refugees, all of them former boat arrivals, could apply for permanent visas. The news was celebrated yet bittersweet. Another 10,000 refugees have been left out and remain in limbo. These include people whose temporary visas, for various reasons, have been refused or are under review. Most fled persecution from countries such as Iran, Afghanistan and Sri Lanka. Some 1100 were medically evacuated here from offshore detention. In June 2023, the last refugee in Nauru was reportedly flown into Brisbane. Around 85 people remain offshore on Papua New Guinea. Taken together, this group, many of whom have lived here for years, still have nowhere to call home.

The need for asylum extends beyond our shores. As of mid-2022, there are 32.5 million refugees worldwide, with over a third (41 per cent) being children. Closer to home, there are 14,000 asylum seekers languishing in Indonesian camps. These are either boat people we have turned back, or asylum seekers we have refused to settle; either way, they are banished to live in limbo without legal rights. 'Suffer or die over there, not here,' we seem to have said to them.

I've seen this suffering up close. My family escaped from Iran after ten of our family members were imprisoned, three of them executed, another one beaten to death in custody. As a child, I'd accompany my parents to visit my jailed uncles. Fast-forward thirty years and I was visiting prisons again, as the ophthalmologist in the detention centres on Manus Island and Nauru. What I saw there quite simply damaged me. Take Mohammad, a 46-year-old Iraqi refugee and father to four girls. He was blinded in one eye after being beaten unconscious when guards and rioters invaded the detention centre. The clinic on Manus lacked the facilities to treat him adequately. Later, he reportedly attempted suicide.

There were children too. A three-year-old from Nepal had conjunctivitis, his eyelids swollen and excoriated. I prescribed eye drops but, on a remote prison-island, it felt like bandaid medicine. Another boy, seven years old and curly-haired, was receiving no schooling – no English classes, nothing. By the time I was his age I was learning to be bilingual. What trajectory were we setting these kids on? I will never forget their faces.

The atmosphere in the detention centres was thick with grief. A ritual developed: at the end of each day, I'd walk to my accommodation, pull the curtains and weep. Since then, this helplessness has swung within me like a pendulum, from a sense of purpose to one of despondency. On the upswings, I'm energised and hopeful, interrogating the ins and outs, the causes and effects, of Australia's asylum policies.

Are they the best we can muster?

I'm left with no doubt that we're capable of more. Before we get to solutions, though, we need to consider the problems.

In 2021 I met Salem Askari, an Afghan refugee living in Perth. He surprised me: a thirty-year-old stonemason in a ute, studying a philosophy degree. In 2012, he fled his homeland after the Taliban murdered his friend. 'A horror movie was unfolding every night,' he told me. He travelled to Indonesia, where he boarded a boat, reaching Christmas Island on 31 March 2013. Like thousands of other asylum seekers, he was granted a temporary visa. Following Minister Giles's announcement, he can apply for a permanent visa.

For the first time, he can apply for a loan, travel overseas and sponsor his wife, whom he hasn't seen in years, to join him. Salem celebrated this news with a friend at a pool hall. 'As a matter of fact, we are not so good at snooker . . . but that night we made every shot!' he recalls, beaming at the memory.

The levity belies Salem's decade-long struggle. As the name suggests, temporary visas don't grant permanent protection, even to 'real' refugees like Salem. At any time, visa holders may be required to leave Australia. Depending on their visa class, others have faced restrictions on work, travel, study, family reunion and access to Medicare and other services. For many there is no financial safety net. Visa holders are kept forever uncertain, living among us yet prevented from putting down meaningful roots. This is a distressing, and sometimes dangerous, way to live.

At times, Salem's temporary status has plunged him into depression. A friend of his on a temporary visa could no longer bear it and died by suicide on Perth's railway tracks. 'He was one of the brightest kids . . . [this situation] kills the spirit of anyone,' Salem reflected. Associate Professor Mary Anne Kenney, a refugee lawyer at Murdoch University, described this to me as 'lethal hopelessness'.

To better understand this, I spoke with Professor Angela Nickerson, Director of the Refugee Trauma and Recovery Program (RTRP) at the University of New South Wales. 'Those on temporary visas have shown significantly greater psychopathology, and thoughts of being better off dead, compared to those with secure visas,' she told me.

Her colleague and the Deputy Director of the RTRP, Dr Belinda Liddell, has conducted brain research on refugees using functional MRI scans. 'Our finding was that post-migration stress was linked with hypersensitivity to perceived threats,' she reported. In other words, past trauma was compounded by stressful experiences in a refugee's new host country, such as visa uncertainty.

The kick in the teeth is that temporary visas don't achieve their own stated goal: to deter boat arrivals. In the first two full years after the Howard government introduced temporary visas (2000 and 2001), the number of people who arrived by boat increased by 88 per cent, from 2939 to 5516 people. In their own problematic way, it was naval turnbacks (where the Australian navy pushed boats back to their point of departure) that more decisively 'stopped the boats'. In their 2021 National Platform, the Labor Party pledged to abolish temporary visas, on the grounds that they 'prevent meaningful settlement'. As of October 2023, however, they have yet to do so.

Another policy that remains intact is offshore processing, despite the fact that for over twenty years, researchers, doctors and others have reported its harmful effects.

In 2016, medical experts from the UN reported that 88 per cent of offshore detainees suffered from mental illness. This was among the highest rate of any surveyed population. Mental health services, meanwhile, were palliative at best. Dr Peter Young, former director of mental health for Manus Island and Nauru, condemned those centres as being 'inherently toxic' and 'akin to torture'. Since January 2018, there have been fifteen suspected or confirmed suicides across onshore and offshore detention. This rate is estimated to be roughly 100 times higher than that in our general community. Doctors and coroners have testified that many of these deaths were preventable.

Children have not been spared. Research published in 2023 shows that almost 90 per cent of children held in off-shore detention on Nauru had physical health problems, such as malnutrition, and almost half (45 per cent) reported suicidal ideation or attempts. Over 2100 critical incidents – including the physical and sexual abuse of children – were revealed by the *Guardian* in the 'Nauru Files'. Katie Robertson, lawyer and Research Fellow at the Peter McMullin Centre on Statelessness, witnessed this. 'I saw babies being nursed in concrete cells, with nowhere for kids to play or crawl,' she recalls. 'We won't know the damage we've done to these children for years to come.'

In 2015, the UN found that aspects of Australia's treatment of asylum seekers violated its Convention Against Torture. In February 2023, Australia joined Rwanda as one of only two countries to obstruct a visit by the UN's Subcommittee on Prevention of Torture.

As with temporary visas, the data reveals that offshore processing doesn't work. Two eras are instructive. First, between 2003 and 2007, the Howard government emptied the centres on Manus and Nauru, while retaining their policy of naval turnbacks. There was no significant uptick in boats (between one and five boats each year). Second, in August 2012, after ceasing naval turnbacks, the Labor government resumed offshore processing. Boat numbers *increased* in the forthcoming months, such that the centres were rapidly filled to capacity. Boat numbers only dropped, and have since stayed down, following the Abbott government's resumption of naval turnbacks in late 2013. In both eras, boat turnbacks had significantly more impact on boat numbers than offshore processing, or any other single policy to 'stop the boats'.

Under conditions of anonymity, a former employee of the Department of Home Affairs verified this with me. Their analysis was that offshore detention persists, despite its empirical lack of efficacy, due to a misguided 'doctrine of necessity'.

While the human costs of this system are incalculable, the financial costs can be enumerated. Analyses of the government's budget papers have revealed a conservative estimate, from 2012 to 2019, of $18.6 billion for offshore processing, onshore detention and boat turnbacks. The average expenditure amounts to $2.66 billion per year. For real-world context, consider that Perth's Fiona Stanley Hospital was built in 2013–14 for $1.76 billion. The opportunity cost of immigration detention, therefore, is analogous to 'one and a half' state-of-the-art hospitals per year.

In 2022–23, despite massive government debt, the spending continues. In January 2023, the Labor government awarded the contract for Nauru's detention centre to MTC (Management and Training Corporation), a private US prisons operator. The three-year contract is for $420 million. Previously, when there were 65 to 70 people left on Nauru, this worked out to an annual cost of $2.1 million per person. With two people reportedly left on Nauru as of 31 August 2023, this figure is now $70 million per person. By contrast, the government's own estimates for allowing someone to live in community detention is $54,798 per year, representing an over 1200-fold cost discrepancy.

The analysis of such evidence demonstrates that, as migration policies go, temporary visas and offshore processing are cruel, ineffective and exorbitantly expensive.

Australians, we can do better than this.

*

Having outlined the problems, let's turn to solutions. These come in two parts, the first addressing the 12,000 former boat arrivals who are stuck in limbo, the second our broader architecture for asylum seekers.

For those left in limbo, in February 2023 Minister Giles stated that 'people who are ultimately found to have been owed protection . . . should be allowed to stay'. It's likely, then, that many in this cohort will settle here. Others will need to appeal for ministerial intervention, whereby the minister can intervene in a case where they feel it is in the public interest to do so. Some will never be allowed to settle here. New Zealand and the US will take a limited number of people who were formerly held on Manus Island and Nauru, but options for the remaining cohort are unclear.

The longer these people remain in limbo, the more they suffer. We owe them prompt, fair resolutions.

'We hope to see swift and practical change in this area,' said Jana Favero, Director of Advocacy at the Asylum Seeker Resource Centre. '[For example] there are thousands of people from Iran and Afghanistan . . . who obviously cannot return home.'

Curtin University's Associate Professor Caroline Fleay suspects that outcomes will be piecemeal. 'There appears to be some movement towards permanency for at least a small number of people with compelling circumstances, and we urgently need to push the government to expand so much more on this.'

Minister Giles's own history may permit cautious optimism. As a solicitor in 2001, he represented refugees aboard the MV *Tampa*. The case became a watershed moment in Australia's history with refugees. 'I think he's the only sitting immigration minister who's ever taken a former immigration minister to court,' Favero told me.

How Giles exercises his ministerial powers – or is permitted to by Labor's right-wing factions – remains to be seen. As Associate Professor Kenny told me, 'It may be encouraging to note that [Minister Giles] is allowing some people from Afghanistan who were initially refused protection to apply again, on the basis that there has been a significant change in their country's situation.'

Let's turn towards the second set of solutions, addressing our broader responses to asylum seekers. In recent years, many policy proposals have been published by expert bodies, including the Kaldor Centre for International Refugee Law, the Asylum Seeker Resource Centre, and the Refugee Council of Australia. These submissions are neither simplistic nor mysterious.

Their thrust may be characterised as a pivot away from reactive, insular tendencies, towards a proactive approach based on a world view of interdependence. They may be boiled down to three aims, and five solutions, which will be explored below, with a focus on strategic themes rather than operating procedures – in other words, prioritising the 'what' and the 'why' over the 'how'.

I will preface this section by conceding that, like it or not, and as evidenced by our federal elections, asylum policies must address the issue of Australian border control. As Independent MP Andrew Wilkie told me, 'The moment the community thinks the government has lost control of its borders, it's finished.' As pragmatists, then, let's start in the Indian Ocean, between Indonesia and northwest Australia.

The First Aim: *to respect Australia's right to govern its borders.*

The First Solution: *keep naval interceptions in place, but replace military turnbacks with good-faith search-and-rescue operations.*

Boat turnbacks are morally and operationally problematic. Their central concern is to push people away, not to ensure their safety or assess their need for protection. As documented by the ABC, and researched in detail by journalists David Marr and Marian Wilkinson (*Dark Victory*, 2003), our navy has at times been instructed to allow refugee boats to sink, before attending to them. In an ABC exclusive report from December 2014, navy personnel admitted that on at least one occasion, this practice led to drownings.

Once intercepted and while still at sea, passengers undergo 'enhanced screening' of their asylum claims. Legal experts have concerns that these conditions are unlikely to constitute a fair hearing and that people may be returned to harm. This has reportedly happened to Vietnamese and Sri Lankan asylum seekers who were repatriated. This breaches our obligations to international law and the Refugee Convention.

Naval officials have described turnbacks as risky for both passengers and their personnel. In 2009, a sabotaged boat exploded off Ashmore Reef, killing five Afghan refugees. Following turn-backs, our duty of care to the boats' passengers appears to evaporate. Boats have reportedly been left without fuel, while others have run aground in Indonesian waters. Bodies of drowned asylum seekers have been left in the water, their retrieval not considered an 'operational priority'. Perhaps reflecting these concerns, the UK Royal Navy in 2022 refused their government's request to conduct turnbacks on the grounds that they were 'inappropriate'.

The counterpoint is that, by the government's measure of zero tolerance on boats, turnbacks can be said to 'work'. While turnbacks have likely prevented some drownings, it's hypocritical to brag about saved lives when we've simply pushed people elsewhere, to suffer or die out of sight. 'Perhaps its fairer to say that neither argument acknowledges the whole picture,' said Madeline Gleeson from the Kaldor Centre for International Refugee Law.

What's needed is a middle ground.

One proposal is good-faith search-and-rescue operations. According to Gleeson, 'search-and-rescue is fundamentally different to turnbacks'. With search-and-rescue, Australia would meet its obligation to the maritime principle of rescuing vessels in distress. Intercepted passengers would be granted asylum procedures on land. Their safe disembarkation and reception, whether to their point of departure or country of origin, would be ensured. Boats could be accompanied to a safe port in Indonesia, as part of a regional protection agreement (more on this in the next section). On being delivered here, passengers could be assisted with accessing safe, lawful asylum procedures for Australia or elsewhere. Passengers would never be returned to a place where they faced a risk of persecution. This determination of risk would be based on information about countries of origin that would be reviewed regularly for accuracy and currency by the Department of Home Affairs.

We'd escort people away, while upholding their dignity. With search-and-rescue operations in place, we could begin to relax our paranoia about border control, and move on.

The Second Aim: *to reduce the incentive for people to get on boats by addressing the root causes of displacement, and through creating additional safe, lawful pathways to protection.*

The Second and Third Solutions: *improve our engagement with our neighbours to promote a regional protection framework, while simultaneously increasing our overall humanitarian intake.*

As with the Covid-19 pandemic, refugee protection is a global issue that needs international cooperation. Australia must shift its focus away from deterrence and detention, towards responsibility-sharing. Contrary to opinions promoted on Sky News, most asylum seekers reach Australia by plane (not boat), from Asian countries of origin that include China, Malaysia and Thailand. In the case of boats, the main country of departure is Indonesia. Here, Indonesia is a transit country, meaning a country through which asylum seekers travel in order to reach a desired destination, in our case Australia. It's sensible, then, to collaborate with these countries, and expand the protection space in our region. This could be a quadruple-win for asylum seekers, for countries of origin, for transit countries, and – in the spirit of enlightened self-interest – for Australia.

To promote regional cooperation, we could bring together the activities of the Department of Foreign Affairs and Trade with those of the Department of Home Affairs (whole-of-government thinking, imagine that!). This is not a new idea. 'If you read the [Expert Panel on Asylum Seekers] report from 2012, this was one of their recommendations,' said Associater Professor Kenny. '[As a result], we resettled people here from Indonesia who had been on boats that had sunk, such as [Hazara man and award winning photojournalist] Barat Ali Batoor.' Through a regional cooperation agreement, Australia could provide humanitarian, development, technical and financial support to countries of origin and first asylum. One vehicle could be the UNHCR's existing 'Emerging Resettlement Countries Joint Support Mechanism', which aims to help countries develop their own refugee systems. Through demonstrating our own commitment, some neighbouring countries might be encouraged to ratify the Refugee Convention, providing further safeguards.

These measures would allow more refugees to settle in countries of first asylum, rather than travel further to Australia or elsewhere. Australia has done it before, when we joined the Comprehensive Plan for Action in the 1970s and '80s. Here, we shared responsibility with Asian countries for people fleeing conflicts in Vietnam and Laos. By 1985, 70,000 refugees from Southeast Asia, mostly from Vietnam, had been resettled in Australia.

Further upstream, we can seek to ameliorate the root causes of displacement, such as persecution, conflict and climate change. There are no simple fixes here, but we can contribute to the capacity of countries to respond to crises. One mechanism is to reverse the cuts made to our foreign aid budget in recent years. As a proportion of GDP, Australia's aid program should be increased from its current level (around 0.2 per cent) to 0.7 per cent, in line with commitments under the UN Sustainable Development Goals, and as the UK, Denmark and Sweden have done.

Increased expenditure on aid could be offset by reduced spending on offshore processing. This would divert resources away from ineffective deterrence towards prevention. Asher Hirsch, Senior Policy Officer at the Refugee Council of Australia, has determined that Australia currently spends $100 million per year on regional cooperation, mostly with Indonesia. 'That's actually not that much money compared to . . . a billion dollars a year [spent] on offshore processing for seventy people,' he noted, citing the number of refugees who remained on Nauru at the time.

For these strategies to work, Australia needs to regain moral authority in the region. Our standing has been undermined by offshore processing and turnbacks, casting us (rightly) as responsibility shirkers. Why should Indonesia collaborate with us when we've dumped 14,000 refugees on them? A principled approach would mend bridges and lay foundations for cooperation. The simplest way to do this is to increase our refugee intake. This can be done in several ways.

First, our Humanitarian Program intake could immediately be increased. While our political leaders claim that we are world leaders in resettlement, the numbers tell a different story. In the ten years prior to Covid, our contribution relative to other countries ranks us in global terms at twenty-fifth overall, twenty-ninth per capita and fifty-fourth by GDP – hardly deserving of self-satisfied backslaps.

For decades, our annual refugee intake has sat at 13,000 to 14,000 people. This is despite a rise in global refugee numbers. At the same time, our economy and population has grown. In relative terms, we've become bigger and richer, while welcoming a smaller share of refugees. Since Covid we've taken fewer still; with 5947 visas issued, our 2020–2021 program was the smallest in forty-five years. We can justify an increased intake by simply saying, 'We can, so we should,' or, to invoke the renowned psychologist Abraham Maslow, 'What a person can be, they should be.'

In August 2023, Minister Andrew Giles announced a modest increase in our quota, up from 17,875 to 20,000 people per year. While the move was welcomed by the refugee sector, it remains short of Labor's own stated goal. In its 2021 National Platform, the

Labor Party stated an aspirational target of 27,000 funded humanitarian entrants per year. Others think we should aim higher. When I spoke to outspoken refugee advocate Julian Burnside QC, he said, 'Make [the intake] 100,000, and no one would bat an eyelid.'

More conservatively, a progressive increase to, say, 32,000 per year, would take us closer to the intake of a comparable high-income country such as Canada, which has pledged a quota of 48,000 people per year. This number should be an indexed percentage of our annual migration intake, and subject to annual review. An additional quota for global crises, such as the Ukraine war and Afghanistan's Taliban takeover, should be provided. A dedicated program for at-risk children should also be considered, as well as access to 'complementary pathways' (other classes of visa), such as skilled migration, study, family reunion and community sponsorship.

Of these, community sponsorship deserves special mention. This is a Canadian idea that we should absolutely emulate. Its Private Sponsorship of Refugees (PSR) program has enabled community groups to resettle refugees for decades: over 350,000 refugees since 1979. A key feature is 'additionality', where sponsored refugee numbers are over and above the government's normal refugee intake. The PSR has been so popular with community sponsors that John McCallum, a former immigration minister, claimed that he was 'the only immigration minister . . . that couldn't bring enough refugees to satisfy the Canadian demand'.

In recent years, Australia has set up its own modest version. In December 2021, our federal government appointed an independent charity to deliver a 'Community Refugee Integration and Settlement Pilot' (CRISP). The charity is Community Refugee

Sponsorship Australia (CRSA), whose CEO, Lisa Button, discussed the scheme with me.

Button recalled her first encounter with this form of sponsorship, during a visit to the UK. A small community in Devon had sponsored some of the first Syrian refugees. 'We sat in this fourteenth-century church with Muslims and Christians and atheists, drinking tea and eating scones and baklava,' she recalled. The Syrian family described their sense of safety, while the Devon locals described how enriching it had been for their community.

CRISP gets my attention for four reasons. First, it's a proven scheme from a country that's comparable to ours. This makes it a low-risk proposition. Second, it engages citizen participation, an under-used cornerstone of democratic policy. Button describes a global sponsorship community who 'really believe in the power of citizens [to] create the communities that we want'. Third, it harnesses the power of human contact – hosts get to know newcomers, up close and personal. (As an Iranian with Aussie in-laws, I know how transformative this is.) Fourth, it provides a structure in which capable, well-meaning people, who may otherwise feel helpless, can contribute to a worthwhile cause.

Compared to the Canadian program, the scale of Australia's CRISP is modest: 1500 refugees over four years. In their 2023 National Conference, the Labor Party declared an aspiration to increase resettlement via complementary pathways (which includes community sponsorship) to 10,000 places and, like Canada, make this additional to the official refugee intake. This pledge was received with cautious optimism, since Labor had pledged an extra 5000 community-sponsored places in their 2021 National Platform and have yet to deliver this. 'I'm hoping [additionality] will happen in the next twelve months,' Button said. 'If we don't fix that . . . I predict we'll struggle to keep running the program.'

So how does this scheme work? I spoke with a sponsor, Lindi Bloch, who is an early childhood educator and mother of two teenagers in eastern Sydney. After some initial caution, she was persuaded by a relative to apply to the CRISP scheme and undergo a short training course with CRSA. She and five other community members were then matched with a Hazara Afghan family of five who had been displaced in Turkey for five years. In November 2022, Bloch met the family for the first time at Sydney Airport, a moment that she recalls as 'exceptionally emotional'. The family spoke no English and, Bloch said laughingly, 'Google Translate doesn't work!' Her group helped the family find a place to live, enrol the children in school, register for Centrelink and Medicare, and open bank accounts.

For twelve months, Bloch's group will assist the family with their expenses through fundraising, while guiding them towards financial independence. CRSA estimates that between $5000 and $25,000 is needed over twelve months per family, with most groups seeking to raise around $12,000. The budget depends on family size, location and the availability of free or in-kind resources. Bloch indicated that the budget for her group was at the higher end of the CRSA's estimate.

Bloch is a committed sponsor who spends five to ten hours each week supporting the family. I asked her what she has learned so far. Prior to sponsorship, she feels she was 'living in a bubble. [Sponsorship] has opened my eyes to knowing and understanding what other people go through and how it is to be a refugee.' She has marvelled at the Afghan family's progress; after just three months, the children speak to her in English. The father has acquired his driver learner's permit and, with his wife, aspires to start an Afghan restaurant. 'Even the grandmother is slowly learning . . . Last weekend she recited the days of the week in English.'

Bloch describes the family's resilience as 'like nothing I have ever seen', and her pride in them is palpable. 'We are only committed to the family for a year, but they will without a doubt be lifelong friends.' Listening to Bloch reminds me of the line by the poet Khalil Gibran, that 'out of suffering have emerged the strongest souls'.

Something remarkable happens following my interview with Bloch. In passing, she tells me that the Afghan grandmother in her sponsored family, whom we shall call Bibi, struggles to see due to her severe cataracts. Bibi can't see the whiteboard in her English classes and barely sees well enough to prepare food, so much so that it's getting her down. It's been difficult to access cataract surgery for her in Sydney, since the public hospital wait time is two to three years. It's also unaffordable, as an uninsured patient, for her to have it done privately. As a practising ophthalmologist, I offer to perform her surgery in Perth at no cost. It will be eminently faster and more affordable for them to travel to Perth for pro bono surgery than to wait or pay for it in Sydney. (This raises a raft of questions about our health system – a topic for another essay!)

The family are nervous. They've not met me and have been in Australia for only four months. The prospect of travelling to another state is daunting for them. I chat by phone with Bibi's son in our shared language of Farsi, explaining the surgery. He sounds reassured and, following this, the family take up the offer. Bloch's group raises the travel funds and two months later I meet Bibi and her son at our practice, the Lions Eye Institute in Perth. Her surgeries with me are successful and at her final check-up, following what's been an anxious wait for Bibi, her son, Bloch and all their families, she's able to see again. It's a powerful moment; I've done this surgery thousands of times and every case is a privilege. But these circumstances are extraordinary and I find myself deeply moved, no doubt in part because of my own family's background as refugees. Later I learn that with her sight restored, Bibi is again preparing tea and food for the family and, based on her vision, would qualify for a driver's licence.

The experience with Bibi, serendipitous and unlikely as it is, reminds me of a comment made by Button. She described how communities seemed to magically produce – almost *divine* – solutions for refugees. She's seen informal conversations ricochet in unexpected directions: a visit to the vet, in one case, where an offhand chat led to a call-out to churches that resulted in long-term accommodation being secured for a refugee family. 'I don't want to get all woo-woo . . . but it almost becomes like a religious experience. We keep saying to [sponsors], "just trust, trust that the universe will deliver if you start talking about it". Something about it taps into the goodness in people. People want to be good people and do good.' Bibi's surgery, a rabbit-out-of-the-hat moment, leaves me – secular and old enough for youth's idealism to have been severely curtailed – with a skerrick of faith in humanity restored. I want to do more.

In Western Australia, CRISP has been championed by Independent MP Kate Chaney. Other Independents, including David Pocock and Zoey Daniel, have echoed this support (more unexpectedly, so has One Nation leader Pauline Hanson). I discussed the appetite for citizen-led change with Chaney. 'I think it's less about changing culture, and it's more about appealing to the best in people,' she reflected. 'A lot of the [political] rhetoric has been based on fear. And I think that we're bigger than that. And if you give people the opportunity to identify with something better than that, they'll take it.'

The Third Aim: *grant asylum seekers fairness, protection and dignity.*

The Fourth and Fifth Solutions: *reform immigration detention and allow asylum seekers to live in the community, with access to work rights and services, while their claims are processed fairly, efficiently and transparently.*

Detention should be a measure of last, not first, resort, with a maximum period of ninety days. Children should never be detained. In Australia, asylum seekers are detained for an average of two years, compared to under ninety days (almost eight-fold less) in Europe. Australia must quit its one-eyed fascination with incarceration, and adopt alternatives such as open centres with reporting requirements, as many European states do.

Offshore detention is a cruel, expensive and unsustainable proposition. We need to permanently end it and process all claims in Australia. When I offered Behrouz Boochani a proverbial magic wand to fix Australia's asylum system, he said, 'Get those people off Manus and Nauru. Do this immediately.' In March 2023, a bill proposing this was voted down in Parliament by the ALP, the Coalition and One Nation. If we won't bring detainees here, we need to promptly settle them elsewhere, and assist them with rebuilding their lives.

Since 2014, Australia has taken excruciatingly long to process claims for boat arrivals. Described in almost Orwellian doublespeak as 'fast-track', this system has set records for procedural slowness.

I discussed this with Dr Daniel Ghezelbash from the Kaldor Centre. 'Very generally, I would say it takes two to three years for the initial claim, and two to three years for judicial review', he said. As slow as this seems, others believe this estimate is optimistic. 'I looked a lot at the stats for this,' said Associate Professor Kenny. 'On average it took up to six years for people to receive their first TPV (Temporary Protection Visa) or SHEV (Safe Haven Enterprise Visa), due to delays in allowing them to lodge their initial applications, coupled with a lack of free legal assistance.' For those denied a visa, judicial review came after this six-year process, adding up to a decade or more for some applicants. The timeframe in comparable countries? 'Switzerland have got their proceedings to forty-five days,' said Ghezelbash. To improve our performance, Ghezelbash says we need better data collection and free legal assistance for applicants.

More broadly, the refugee sector has unanimously called for 'fast-track' to be abolished and replaced with fair hearings that comply with international standards. These processes should be transparent, as in Canada and France, which have performed independent reviews of their asylum procedures and made the findings public.

It is noteworthy that our mistreatment of asylum seekers is reserved mainly for boat arrivals. Far more asylum seekers arrive by plane – over 95,000 people since 2017 – without attracting public attention. This invokes the irony that, as a nation colonised by boats, we're sensitive to history repeating itself. As I have observed in a poem, 'he who invades, fears history the most' ('White Noise', 2016).

Taking this further, we may ask, 'What is the national psyche that reacts disproportionately to boats?' António Guterres, a former UN High Commissioner for Refugees, has framed this as Australia's 'floating obsession'. Let us peer, then, *beneath* the nuts and bolts of policy, and inspect its cultural underpinnings: behold, the belly of the beast.

Julie Macken has researched these questions. Macken is a former journalist and political consultant turned PhD candidate at Western Sydney University. Her subject is Australia's treatment of refugees or, in Macken's words, 'How has Australia become a country that tortures asylum seekers?' Her interviewees have included psychiatrists, some of whom have treated asylum seekers for decades. These experts, capable of analysing the impact of detention, have concluded that it constitutes a form of torture.

Macken's thesis is that Australia has become a 'melancholic torturer', with roots extending back to our dispossession of Aboriginal people. She elaborated on these views, starting with offshore camps.

'What space do the camps hold for us?' she asked. Her premise is that communities have a 'shared psychic landscape'. Within this, physical structures, such as a camp or prisons, are created by the collective psyche – they exist literally but also metaphorically. Macken's view is confronting. '[The camps] are psychotic pockets that are not connected to our conscious mind . . . the kind of repository of all our abject fear and anxiety . . . and debasement of human beings.'

In Macken's estimation, these 'psychotic pockets' are rooted in Australia's colonial history. Here, she mirrors the work of Behrouz Boochani, Omid Tofighian and Moones Mansoubi (*Freedom, Only Freedom*, 2022). They have argued that Australia's 'prison archipelago' is neither novel nor rare. Rather, it is an extension of Australia's settler-colonial history, the modern face of the White Australia policy, the penal colony, mission and outstation.

Left unchecked, the cycle spirals until we're numb to the atrocities of asylum seekers drowning and children in detention. 'We are impoverished by this, as every kind of half-dead bully is impoverished,' Macken added.

In the therapeutic model, psychoses are treated by naming them, with skeletons walked out of the closet. 'This allows [psychoses] to be reintegrated, so we can actually deal with the material.' Macken believes Australia did this in the 1970s, when Gough Whitlam renounced White Australia and Malcolm Fraser accepted 50,000 refugees from Vietnam. '[We were] treating people who came here by boat decently, because we were in touch with the fact that *we* came here by boat.'

For me, this evokes Robert Frost's 'the best way out is always through'. The poet's ideal is that truth and courage will deliver restitution. But how might this be achieved at a national level?

Macken feels a Royal Commission is warranted. This notion is shared by the Australian Greens, Catholics for Refugees, some Independent MPs and refugee groups. Following an anticipated refusal from Labor, Macken predicts the campaign would turn to a public petition. This is reminiscent of the Uluru Statement; after its initial dismissal by the Coalition government, it became a grassroots movement. The psychic links between Aboriginal dispossession and asylum seekers, it seems, are pervasive.

Zaki Haidari, a Hazara Afghan refugee and advocate for Amnesty International, agrees with the need for a public reckoning. 'In particular the Australian government . . . they have to acknowledge and take responsibility . . . the damage that this whole cruelty has done to refugees and their families.'

Just as calling for a Royal Commission is ambitious, so too

is the need for reparations real. I permit myself a speculation, an imagined future where a prime minister – perhaps even our first Aboriginal PM – delivers the 'National Apology to Asylum Seekers', expressing our regret and offering recompense. Hypothetical, yes, but as one who walks in two worlds, I view an honest reckoning with refugees as being integral to Australia's long-term interests in the interdependent Asia–Pacific region, as well as to our budgetary sustainability and our cultural enrichment. Perhaps, even, to our national pride in being a redeemed, compassionate people.

The refugee crisis isn't going away. We can't aspire to let the whole world in, but nor can we stonewall it forever. Failure to act will lead to the suffering and deaths of more refugees and boomerang on us by destabilising our region and creating long-term economic costs. With much at stake, the question is less whether we're up for this challenge and more whether we can afford not to try.

Our only real choice, as Frost knew, is to face it head on: to forgo insularity in favour of policies of interdependence, to redirect expenditure from detention to measures of prevention, and to shift towards protecting rather than punishing vulnerable people. We've done this before, through significant refugee intakes after World War II, after the Indochina crisis of the 1970s, and after the Tiananmen Square massacre of 1989, to name a few examples. All told, Australia has resettled over 950,000 refugees since 1947, including the likes of my family. Where would you be without us, and us without you?

As we've acted before, so can we act again, knowing bone-deep that our long-term survival is contingent on that of others. Let our invitations be orderly, let them be strategic – and let them be bold.

Fighting On

Fighting On

Introduction by
Matthew Drummond

There's a saying in newsrooms that good stories are like earthworms: they disappear out of view, but eventually they come back up to the surface. It's a reminder that for all the focus on newness in journalism – on finding fresh yarns and breaking ground – there are stories that deserve to be revisited. Indeed, stories that might be forgotten are sometimes all the more compelling.

After the Taliban took Kabul in 2021 and cemented their return to power in Afghanistan, newspapers and magazines were filled with news and features about the plight of Afghan refugees and those trapped in the country who had tried to flee. And then those stories petered out. Liz Gooch has swum against the tide and kept returning to this story, to yield a series of long-form pieces exploring the lives of Afghan women.

This feature explores the extraordinary lengths to which a woman, Zahra, who was once a member of the country's national judo team, goes to train in Taliban-controlled Afghanistan. Gooch contrasts Zahra's story with the narrative of another Afghan athlete, Fatima, who managed to flee the Taliban and is now living in Melbourne, where she trains in taekwondo. The writer found both women, whose stories are told for the first time in this feature, through contacts she has made from her previous reporting on the lives of Afghan women, which has been published in *The Saturday Paper*, *The Weekend Australian* and *Good Weekend*.

Gooch sets both Fatima's and Zahra's stories against the bigger picture of whether the International Olympic Committee will ban Afghanistan from the 2024 Olympics in Paris. The IOC's charter states that it is the organisation's role 'to act against any form of discrimination' and 'to encourage and support the promotion of women in sport at all levels'. As Gooch writes, the Taliban has effectively erased women from public life. And yet, as at October 2023, over two years after the Taliban's takeover, the IOC was still to make a decision. Friba Rezayee, who made history in Athens in 2004 as one of the first women to represent Afghanistan at the Olympics, tells Gooch she's shocked that the IOC has continued to meet with Afghanistan's rulers. 'It was very clear what the Taliban are capable of,' she says. 'They basically declared war against women in Afghanistan. This is gender apartheid. And the IOC still chose to engage with them.'

That point marks the fulcrum of a piece that explores what's truly at stake – the physical and mental strength that playing sport gives to girls and women. Whether training in secret in Afghanistan or amid the pressures of building a new life in a foreign country, these two women demonstrate the power of women's sport. And how poetic, given what they are fighting against, that both are training in martial arts.

Fighting On

Liz Gooch

A YOUNG WOMAN'S BODY HITS THE FLOOR WITH A LOUD THWACK. As she gets to her feet, her opponent grabs her forearm, heaves her onto her back, and lifts her feet off the ground before flinging her down again. 'Very good,' says her coach. The two women break apart for a ten-second rest before coming back together for another round, their breathing becoming more laboured as they repeat the drill.

The fighters freeze. One woman's leg hangs midair, poised ready to strike. Suddenly, the image on my computer screen goes black.

Before her internet connection dropped out, I'd been watching Zahra, one of Afghanistan's top judo athletes, grapple with her training partner. Once a week, she pulls on white pants and a long-sleeved white top, and ties a black belt around her waist. She props her phone up on the floor in front of her and logs onto an online training session, in the privacy of the two-room house she shares with her husband, baby and in-laws. Her coach video calls from Norway.

Zahra was a member of the Afghan national judo team, and has long dreamed of representing her country at the Olympics. But in Taliban-controlled Afghanistan, this is the only way she can train.

With women banned from playing sport and from going to gyms or parks, I can't tell you Zahra's real name, or where she lives. She fears that if the Taliban knew who she was, or if she was caught training, she could be imprisoned, tortured or even killed. 'I'm scared to go outside because of the Taliban,' says the 26-year-old.

All vestiges of her old life vanished as the Taliban began their crackdown on women's rights after seizing control of the country in 2021. 'I used to be one of those people who were outside all the time,' she says. 'I would leave home early in the morning and come home late in the evening. Now I'm just trapped at home.'

More than 11,000 kilometres away in Melbourne, energetic music blares as another martial arts training session gets underway. Inside the Combat Institute of Australia's National Performance Centre, the best teenage taekwondo athletes in Victoria are sparring beneath a giant mural that proclaims 'Australian Fighting Spirit' in green and gold lettering. Nimbly bouncing forwards and backwards, girls balance on one leg like storks, before pouncing at their opponents as a tiger would its prey.

When the girls take a break and the boys take up their positions, one of the smallest girls, Fatima, remains on the mats. With her dark ponytail dangling out the back of her red helmet, she goes another round with one of the boys. Fatima eventually takes a break, throws her helmet onto the floor and drops her compact frame down effortlessly into the splits, her face shining with sweat on a Saturday morning in August, 2022. It is this kind of work ethic that got her selected for the development squad. 'She had this X factor about her,' says coach Ryan Carneli.

That X factor was first recognised in Fatima's native Afghanistan. At the age of thirteen, she was named her country's best junior female fighter and selected for the national junior taekwondo team. When the Taliban seized power, she feared her fighting days were over. Unwilling to imagine a life without the sport she'd come to love, Fatima says she knew immediately what she needed to do. 'I decided I had to leave,' she says.

Two weeks later, Fatima packed a backpack, pulled on a hijab she'd rarely worn before, said goodbye to her family, boarded a bus, and headed off into the darkness. She was fourteen years old.

It's often said that sport has the power to transform lives. Nelson Mandela thought it could even change the world. For Afghan girls like Zahra and Fatima, sport *had* changed their world. In Afghanistan's patriarchal society, it brought them not just physical but also mental strength, confidence and independence. But their lives were violently thrown off course after Taliban fighters poured into Kabul in 2021.

As the international community watched on, the Taliban began their fully fledged assault on women's rights almost immediately. In what United Nations experts say could amount to crimes against humanity and 'gender apartheid', the Taliban has effectively erased women from public life, controlling almost every aspect of their lives: what they must wear, where they can go, banning them from high schools and universities and most jobs, and bringing back brutal punishments like flogging.

Sport, which the Taliban considers dishonourable for women, was an early target. Suddenly half of the population was no longer free to kick a ball, shoot hoops or whack a cricket ball.

This is a story of two young women with mirrored lives, who now live in very different worlds. Both have been transformed through sport. Both have felt their confidence soar, and then watched their worlds shatter. One of them cannot win, no matter how skilled a fighter she becomes. She cannot even take part. The other has freedom but can no longer represent the country of her birth. And both stand at the core of a dilemma confronting the International Olympic Committee: is it better to engage with the Taliban in the hope of convincing them to reverse their ban on women's sport? Or should Afghanistan simply be barred from competing at the Paris 2024 Olympics?

Zahra was fourteen years old the first time she stepped onto a judo mat. Already a keen basketball and volleyball player, she decided to sign up for judo after representatives from the Afghan Judo Association came to her school to recruit female athletes. After only a few training sessions, she began competing. And when she won her first gold medal in a local competition, she was hooked. 'I wanted to continue because it made me realise my own strength and power,' she tells me over a video call.

It was 2012, and Afghan girls like Zahra were enjoying a level of freedom that had been denied to the previous generation. The Taliban ruled Afghanistan from 1996 until 2001, when they were removed by a US-led coalition after the September 11 attacks. During their reign, they became notorious for their treatment of women, who were forbidden from going out in public without a male guardian and subject to stoning for alleged crimes like adultery. School was only for boys.

After the US ousted the Taliban, girls' schools reopened and more women joined the workforce, becoming politicians, police officers and lawyers. And, gradually, girls began taking up sports like soccer, volleyball, cycling and martial arts. National teams were formed and female athletes began travelling overseas to compete.

In 2004, Afghanistan sent women to the Olympics for the first time. Zahra was then six years old. When she took up judo, her coach spoke of the opportunities sport could bring. 'He constantly told us, "You have the power, the ability. Train hard and become someone, become the champion you want. If you train hard, you can travel, you can participate at international competitions and you can be a champion and participate at the Olympic Games."'

But Afghanistan remained a deeply conservative society, and for Zahra, that encouragement was not replicated at home. 'My mother never liked the idea of women doing sport . . . She always told me that sport is not for women,' she recalls.

Even when Zahra won competitions, she says her mother told her, 'It's not going to serve you better for the long term, because this is Afghanistan. No matter what a strong person you become, you can never be independent because you're always going to need men in your life and you're always going to be dependent on them, so all these activities are going to be useless for you.'

Her mother wasn't the only one who wanted her to stop training; her brother offered to pay her money to quit sport and stay home. 'But I did whatever I wanted and I am who I am now because I continued my sport,' she says.

By the time Zahra was in her early twenties, her life revolved around training, competing and studying. Three days a week, she would wake early and catch a minivan, then a bus, to the Afghan Olympic Centre in Kabul, where she would study English in the mornings, then spend the afternoon training before going to night school. She'd missed a couple of years of high school when her family moved out of the capital, but was determined to finish her education.

In a country where arranged marriages are common, Zahra was relieved when her family agreed to let her marry a man she loved. 'It was my choice. It was a love marriage,' she says.

Right from the start of their relationship, Zahra made it clear to her husband-to-be that for her, sport was non-negotiable. 'I told him strictly, "If you don't respect me and my rules, this is not going to work," and we made an agreement that he's not going to interfere and he will support me whatever I do,' she says.

After marrying at the age of twenty-three, Zahra moved into her in-laws' house and her husband kept his promise. What she didn't factor in was that the life she'd so carefully built could be torn apart by men she'd never met.

On 15 August 2021, Zahra watched in shock as television networks broadcast footage of armed Taliban fighters streaming into Kabul. They took over the presidential palace, and news broke that then Afghan president Ashraf Ghani had fled the country.

As a member of the national team, Zahra had been interviewed on television and was active on social media. 'Our pictures were on the internet, and we became obvious targets to the Taliban,' she says.

Desperate to flee, Zahra sent a text message to Friba Rezayee, a former Afghan Olympian who had moved to Canada years earlier. She had been helping promote Zahra as an up-and-coming leader in the sport. But now she told Zahra to hide her medals, her certificates. Her proudest moments, once celebrated, had become dangerous liabilities to be protected at all costs. Zahra was 'in danger of retaliation from the Taliban because she played sport, because she was a public figure,' says Friba. 'She played sport without a hijab.'

Desperate to get Zahra and other young women she knew out of Afghanistan before the last foreign troops left, Friba frantically got to work, compiling a spreadsheet of dozens of names – judo athletes, volleyball players, university students. After reams of paperwork and countless phone calls to her contacts, Friba managed to add Zahra's and her husband's names to a US military flight list. About two weeks after the takeover, Zahra covered herself in a full-length burqa, and the young couple headed to Kabul International Airport. There they plunged into the massive crowd swarming towards the gates. For hours they tried to fight their way through to the plane. But it was no use. 'We couldn't [get through] because of the chaos, so we returned home,' Zahra says.

It was past midnight in Vancouver when the news reached Friba. 'I wanted to scream at the top of my lungs,' she says. 'I was trying to evacuate them to safety . . . but we failed.' By the time the last foreign military flights took off, some of the university students Friba had been working with had been evacuated, but dozens of people on her list remained behind.

Friba Rezayee knows the fear of being targeted as an Afghan woman who dared to play sport. A judo athlete, she was one of the two women who made history competing for Afghanistan at the 2004

Olympics in Athens. 'It's the greatest thing that ever happened to me,' she says. 'I was honoured to do that for other Afghan women and to become a pioneer for Afghan women's sport . . . so that I could start the revolution.'

But the exhilaration of competing on the world stage at the age of eighteen vanished when Friba returned home to Kabul. From the moment her selection in the Olympic team was announced, she had begun receiving death threats. When she returned from Athens, these threats escalated and she was forced to go into hiding. In 2005, she fled to Pakistan, and was eventually granted asylum in Canada in 2011.

Friba remembers the crushing disappointment of having her sporting career ripped away when she was at her peak, and the pain of having to flee her homeland. 'It's devastating,' she says from her home in Vancouver. 'I cannot describe and express in words how it feels.'

A plain-spoken advocate who pulls no punches, Friba, who's now aged thirty-seven, is angry that the international community has not done more to help female Afghan athletes, who she believes have been 'left to the mercy of the Taliban'. She sends me a photograph she received via WhatsApp in mid-2022. It's a close-up shot showing a purple bruise staining the skin on an arm. The photograph came from a national judo athlete, who told Friba that a Taliban guard had hit her with an AK-47 after finding her in a secret gym for women in June 2022, about ten months after the ban on sport had been announced. 'She said there were two Taliban fighters. They saw her first and she was just getting ready to get out, but they got her at the entrance and hit her,' Friba recalls. The Taliban fighter told her never to come back to the gym.

A few months later, Friba helped the woman flee to Pakistan, along with another member of the national team. But she says with the war in Ukraine dominating the world's attention, finding sanctuary abroad has become even harder. 'The world doesn't care about Afghan women,' she says.

Athletes continue to contact her via social media, email and phone. 'I constantly hear desperate messages, nonstop messages crying for help, begging me to help them leave the country, begging me to help them to go back to training centres and to have access to any sports facilities,' she says. 'I tell them, "Hang in there, there's going to be hope," because there has to be. Hope is the only thing that is keeping them alive.'

In the wake of the Taliban's ban on women playing sport, Afghan men's teams continued to play international matches in sports like cricket and soccer. But as the Taliban's crackdown on women intensified throughout 2022 and 2023, calls for Afghanistan to be barred from all international sports events grew louder.

When the Taliban was last in power, Afghanistan was barred from attending the Sydney 2000 Olympics. The IOC's charter states that it is the organisation's role 'to act against any form of discrimination affecting the Olympic Movement' and 'to encourage and support the promotion of women in sport at all levels'.

The IOC first met with the newly appointed Afghan sports authorities in November 2021, two months after the deputy head of the Taliban's cultural commission, Ahmadullah Wasiq, told SBS News that women would no longer be allowed to play sport.

In a statement issued after their second meeting in June 2022, the IOC said Afghan representatives had committed to fielding a mixed team at the Paris Games and reiterated their commitment to the Olympic Charter, in particular the right of women and girls to practise sport safely without discrimination.

Back in Afghanistan, there was little evidence that the Taliban was honouring this commitment. By this time, most girls had been banned from secondary schools for almost a year, many women had been forced to stop working, and the Taliban had ordered them to cover their faces in public. By the end of 2022, women would also be banned from universities, from gyms and parks, and be prohibited from working for non-government organisations.

The IOC issued a statement in December 2022, stipulating that for Afghanistan to compete at the Paris 2024 Olympics, the Taliban would need to ensure that girls and women have safe access to sport. The IOC also said that the Afghan team must include athletes living in Afghanistan as well as those living abroad.

Seven months later, in July 2023, the IOC issued formal invitations to 203 countries to compete at the Paris Games. Afghanistan was one of them.

The IOC said it would continue to monitor the situation in Afghanistan and that the specific details for Afghanistan's participation in the Paris Games had not yet been decided.

At a meeting in Mumbai in October 2023, James Macleod, the IOC's director of Olympic Solidarity and National Olympic Committee Relations, said there had been 'ongoing conversations and discussions with the Afghan government authorities since that regime change and we've been insisting on removing existing barriers from the government that hinder women and young girls from accessing sport opportunities in the country. The IOC executive board took a very clear position on this in December 2022, and we have reiterated that position with the government authorities on numerous occasions.'

Rights advocates could not fathom that nine months before the Paris Olympics, there had been no official ban on Afghanistan taking part in the world's biggest sporting event.

Minky Worden, Director of Global Initiatives at Human Rights Watch, says there is 'literally no way' the IOC could avoid banning Afghanistan from the Paris Games. 'You can't say we're in favour of gender equality and then welcome a government that chooses to ban all sport, education and work for women,' she says.

Friba Rezayee was shocked that the IOC even met with Afghanistan's new rulers. 'It was very clear what the Taliban are capable of,' she says. 'They basically declared war against women in Afghanistan. This is gender apartheid. And the IOC still chose to engage with them.'

The Taliban have rejected criticisms of their treatment of women. Supreme leader Haibatullah Akhundzada released a message in June 2023 saying that 'necessary steps have been taken for the betterment of women as half the society in order to provide them with a comfortable and prosperous life according to the Islamic Shariah,' Associated Press reported.

If Afghanistan is eventually banned from the 2024 Olympics, it won't be the only country missing when the cauldron is lit at the opening ceremony. The war in Ukraine has cost both Russia and Belarus the opportunity to send teams to the Paris Games. In July 2023, the IOC announced that the two countries would not receive formal invitations to the games. However, athletes with Russian or Belarusian passports may still be able to compete as neutral athletes. The IOC said it would 'take this decision at the appropriate time'.

Calls for a total ban on Russian and Belarusian athletes have only grown louder as the war in Ukraine has raged on. Ukrainian President Volodymyr Zelensky was unequivocal when he addressed a meeting of sports ministers from thirty-five countries. 'If there's an Olympics sport with killings and missile strikes, you know which national team would take the first place,' he was quoted as saying by Reuters in February 2023. 'Terror and Olympism are two opposites; they cannot be combined.'

Sport is often proclaimed to be a unifying force for peace that transcends war and politics, but the Olympic history books are littered with bans and boycotts. Germany and its allies were banned from competing after World War I, and then again after World War II. A generation of athletes from South Africa missed out on the Olympics, in one of the longest bans ever imposed. The country was prohibited from sending a team for thirty-two years, from 1960 until 1992, due to its apartheid policies.

Far from the boardrooms where IOC decisions are made that affect their futures, Afghan athletes are getting on with their lives, at home and abroad.

On a Thursday afternoon in February 2023, students begin trickling out the gates of Cranbourne Secondary College into a stifling heat blanketing Melbourne. It's been six months since I met Fatima during taekwondo training, and I'm here to see how she's adjusting to her new life. As teenagers splinter off in various directions, some young couples hold hands, others clutch phones.

Fatima appears, wearing a short-sleeved, checked tunic over black tights and platform sneakers, her straight dark hair hanging below her shoulders. It's just a few weeks before her sixteenth birthday. Here, she's just another schoolgirl walking to the bus stop after classes are done for the day. It's a scene that would be impossible had she remained in Afghanistan. Fatima chats to a friend as we board a bus to go and meet her coach, and I wonder how many of her classmates know how she got here.

Her journey began with a message over social media. After the Taliban seized control of Afghanistan, a member of the national women's taekwondo team contacted Ali Rahimi, an Afghan-Australian taekwondo coach and an international referee. Ali phoned Heather Garriock, chief executive of Australian Taekwondo and a former member of the Australian Women's Football team, who then asked former Socceroos captain and refugee advocate Craig Foster how they could help the athletes. Working with immigration lawyers, the group helped secure offshore humanitarian visas and arranged for the evacuation of seven female taekwondo athletes, including Fatima.

They took an overnight bus from Kabul, passing through Taliban checkpoints on an eleven-hour journey to the Pakistan border. But the Taliban guards refused to let them pass. The athletes waited for three days until they received letters from the Australian High Commissioner in Pakistan. When they returned to the border, Fatima says they again argued with the guards, showing them their Australian visas and letters, and eventually they were allowed to cross into Pakistan. 'They were like, "Just shut up and go,"' she recalls.

They travelled to the Pakistani capital, Islamabad, with staff from the Australian High Commission, then flew to Darwin, spending two weeks in a quarantine hotel before moving on to Melbourne. Ali remembers meeting them the day after they arrived there. 'I was like, "Ah, thank God, they are here now,"' he says.

Fatima enrolled in an English course and, six months after she arrived, started attending high school. She trains four days a week with Ali, who was appointed her guardian. She has competed in events around Australia, from Brisbane to Bendigo, where she won a bronze medal in the 49–52 kilogram junior division at the 2022 National Championships.

Fatima says she's 'so happy' she can compete in Australia. 'I came here for taekwondo. It was the only reason I came here,' she says. 'There's a lot of people in Afghanistan, they've trained for five, ten years and now they're told they can't train or go to competitions.'

She wants to go to university to become a social worker, and often helps organise activities for refugee children during school holidays.

With training cancelled the day we meet due to the heat, we head to Fatima's new home – a room in a two-storey building on a quiet residential street east of Melbourne's CBD. She previously lived with Ali and his family, but recently moved into this student accommodation.

When you enter her room, the first thing you notice is the life-sized teddy bear sitting at the foot of her bed. Medals adorn a small round table, where there's another teddy bear, this one dressed in a miniature taekwondo uniform. Photos of Fatima with medals around her neck are stuck on the wall above her desk.

There's a small kitchenette but Fatima usually grabs fast food for dinner on her way home from training. She says she doesn't know how to cook, and misses her mum's home-made food.

It takes her an hour and a half to get to and from school each day, taking a bus, then a train. On training days, she doesn't get home until about 9.30 pm. She spends other evenings studying in a local library. Fatima has made friends with some of the students she lives with in the dormitory, but says the holidays can be lonely when most of the others head home. 'I'm not living here, I just come here to sleep,' she says.

This is a girl who is used to working hard and pushing through barriers – both physical and societal. In Afghanistan, she trained six days a week. On Sundays, her only day off, she'd go running with teammates on the outskirts of Kabul. When a boy kicked her in the face and broke her nose during practice, Fatima, then twelve years old, was back at training the next day.

But now, on top of school and sport, she must deal with the daily challenges of life in a foreign country. She must budget the money she receives from the government to pay for rent, food and other expenses. A case manager assigned by a refugee support group helps her navigate the necessities of life in Australia, like Medicare. She also has to meet with the immigration lawyer who is handling her family's refugee application. She says they haven't been able to give her any indication if or when her family may be allowed to come to Australia.

Since we last met, she's cut back on training from six sessions a week to four, and now spends Saturdays taking Persian language classes, one of her school subjects, instead of training with the state development squad. 'I need more time to study,' she says. As soon as she gets a job, she plans to send money back to her family. Caught between childhood and an adulthood that's been forced upon her, the pressures of forging a new life, so far from family, seem to weigh heavily. But Fatima is pragmatic. 'I have to accept it. I don't have any other choice,' she says matter-of-factly.

Asked whether she still dreams of the Olympics, Fatima says she'll continue training hard and take the opportunities on offer. But, she adds, the standard of competition is much higher in Australia than in her homeland. 'I will try to make it, instead of dreaming,' she says. 'I was confident in Afghanistan but not here . . . I have a lot of stress.'

Fatima left everything she knew and everyone she loved behind because of taekwondo. But for now, her options for competing at the highest levels of her sport are limited. She is not eligible for international competitions like World Championships or the Olympics, because she is not yet an Australian citizen. Fatima says she'll apply for citizenship as soon as she becomes eligible in 2026.

Athletes who remain in Afghanistan, like Zahra, can only dream of the daily freedoms afforded to those who managed to flee. After the Taliban took over, the parameters of Zahra's life shrank. 'I went into hiding because I didn't want to be seen by the Taliban,' she says, sitting on her couch wrapped in a winter jacket. Wiping tears from her eyes, she describes the impact of losing everything she'd worked for. 'I didn't want to live anymore,' she says quietly. 'I was having very bad thoughts about ending my life. It's very upsetting, because we worked very hard. All our achievements and gains for the last fifteen years, they're all gone.'

Zahra's days took on a new structure within the confines of her home – cooking, doing housework, constantly feeding wood into the stove to warm their house during the cold winters. And almost six months after the Taliban takeover, she gave birth to a baby boy. In the months that followed, she tried to regain her fitness, doing push-ups, sit-ups and running up the stairs to the rooftop with her husband. Then, in December 2022, Zahra received a message from her old coach, who was now in Norway. He wanted to know if she'd like to train online. 'That made me very happy and I promised him that whatever it takes, I will do it,' says Zahra. She also began following exercise videos on YouTube every morning before cooking breakfast for her family.

But she fears even training behind the walls of her home could bring danger. Up to six girls used to train at Zahra's house, but one day, she says, a Taliban soldier yelled at the girls as they approached her house, demanding to know what they were doing. They told him they were going to a family lunch, but he ordered them to leave and not come back.

Zahra suspects somebody had followed the girls and reported them. 'If any group of women come together to train or they have a meeting, somebody notices and will report that to the Taliban,' she says. 'We decided that each time we do training, we will choose different locations so we don't draw attention from the Taliban.'

Even still, the women are often too afraid to come together. On the day I watch their online session, only one other woman has come to train with Zahra.

In recent weeks, Zahra has been too afraid to leave her home. The day before we speak, she ventured outside for the first time in three weeks. Describing the dread she feels every time she goes beyond her front door, she says, 'When I go outside, I cover myself from head to toe. I don't show even an inch of skin on my body, fearing that if they notice they will beat me.'

She is still trying to find a way to get to a country where she can train and study freely, but she wonders if perhaps it is her destiny to remain in Afghanistan. She says the fifteen days she spent in Japan on a training camp in 2019 were 'the greatest days' of her life. 'Sometimes I think that I may have used all my happy days . . . and I'll never have them again,' she says.

Her relatives, who never wanted her to play sport in the first place, now tell her that all her training was for nothing. 'It's very upsetting and makes me really angry,' she says. 'Because I wasn't able to get out of the country like other athletes, that gives them more reason to harass me and to prove their point to me: "Look, you didn't succeed in sport. See, we told you sport's not useful or helpful in any capacity for women. Look at your life now."'

But when I ask if she still aspires to compete at the Olympics, her smile returns and the words come like rapid fire. 'One hundred per cent I want that,' she says. 'I want to be able to go to training camp, work hard day and night, and prove to those people who said to me that sport's not for women, prove them wrong. I want to win a medal and bring back the medal and show it to them. Hey, you were wrong, I was right. Look, I won!'

Her dream, it seems, remains intact. Her determination is undimmed, beyond the reach of those imposing their will on her life. Donning her white uniform within the confines of her own home is now her stubborn act of resistance, her protest against her oppressors.

Amid the constant fear of having to hide who she is, Zahra clings tight to these tiny fragments of her old life. She refuses to extinguish the spark that has burned since her first taste of victory as a fourteen-year-old who rejected anyone who told her sport was not for women. 'It gives me an identity,' she says. 'I don't regret a moment of it.'

Postscript

In September 2023, Zahra and her husband moved to Iran, leaving their son in Afghanistan with her parents. She found a job in a clothing factory and is saving money to apply for a visa to another country, such as Australia, the US or Canada. She hopes to reunite with her son soon and resume training. Zahra still hopes to go to the Olympics one day.

On Cups

Introduction by Ceridwen Dovey

Cups are everyday objects that hold enormous meaning.

I had not thought much about cups and everything they signify until I began to work with Penelope. I was immediately struck by her take on these objects, how she rescues them from being overlooked or ignored as insignificant. Object histories are a rewarding way of eavesdropping on the present and the past, but the lowly cup had not, until now, been much used as an object with which to think or feel about humans. Penelope's essay changes that.

Penelope's background as a design writer has honed her ability to write about objects – and about the interior spaces in which most people pass their daily lives. In this essay, though, she has been courageous in stepping quite far outside her writerly comfort zone, taking a more unusual and creative look at the cup, beyond its relevance as a design object. Her essay moves across cities and countries, between centuries and millennia, from the personal to the political, but always with a lightness of touch.

This gentle approach was enabled by her ability to listen to the stories that objects hold within them, and to the stories that humans hold on to about objects. In researching her essay, Penelope drew on her own experiences and also reached out to establish meaningful connections with others, asking them to trust her with their stories of significant cups. They did, and this essay is the proof. At the heart of any worthwhile journalism is this skill of deep listening to others – tuning in to their narratives, and then shaping and crafting them, as a potter does with a lump of clay, into something with clean lines and rounded curves, something that is a genuine pleasure to read.

There is a spirit of playful experimentation that animates this essay, with Penelope setting a slightly different tone or mood in each short piece. Put together, as fragments scavenged from (mostly forgotten) histories, the whole essay becomes like a cup that we – as readers – are putting back together.

By focusing on the cups that have endured over time, whether due to their robust materiality or being kept 'alive' by the meaning given to them by their human owners, Penelope asks us to consider what a world in which all objects are cared for, re-used, passed down over time, repaired when they break, kept cycling and recycling in human exchange might look like. When she first started out, she had wanted this essay to be more overtly about sustainable object design and climate change. After our first discussion, as she began to focus only on cups and our relationships with them, that message became more subtly embedded in the essay. Once she had let go of any concern that this focus was too small, the bigger meanings came flooding in.

In tribute to Penelope asking people to reflect on their own favourite cups, here is the story of mine. It's mottled dusky pink, with some kind of gold-looking metal around the rim and glazed on the handle. I stole it from the graduate student kitchenette as a memento on the day I decided to drop out of my PhD, fifteen years ago. Recently, in an absent-minded moment, I microwaved the cup to heat up some milk, and saw the sparks fly as the metal met the wrong kind of waves. The gold rim suddenly went silver, and probably now leaks toxins. I don't care. I still drink from it every morning.

On Cups

Penny Craswell

1

THERE IS SOMETHING COMFORTINGLY INTIMATE ABOUT A CUP.
There is perhaps no other object to which we touch our lips more
often. Fierce, irrational attachments form to favourite cups or
mugs. If they break or go missing, we mourn their loss. They are
vessels that we carry with us through life – or rather, that carry *us*
through the long days and dark nights of our lives.

Kiln-fired pottery cups may shatter, but they do not degrade.
Fragments of cups thousands of years old persist in the earth's
layers, tiny reminders that people, whose languages and ways of life
are now unimaginable to us, once upon a time sat down to drink
from cups.

When archaeologists dredged the riverbeds at the bottom
of Amsterdam's canals between 2003 and 2012, they uncovered
700,000 objects. Everything you can think of is there, including a
large number of ceramic fragments.

Sample of ceramic findings, Below the Surface project, City of Amsterdam, Monuments and Archaeology

They stitched together a vast image of their findings and published it online. You can zoom in or out of it at will. It is mesmerising. As you scan the brightly patterned ceramic shards, it is not always possible to tell a cup from a mug, a teapot from a jug. There are bits of plates, bowls, chamber-pots.

There's a shard from a beaker dated from 2400–2000 BCE. Brown and earthy, it is decorated with subtle cross-hatching. This cup was made by one of the early Bronze Age 'beaker people' who originated from this part of the Netherlands, so named because they were buried with their bell-shaped beakers.

There's a delicate porcelain teacup from the mid-nineteenth century, with a small handle and enamel glaze. Letters have been painted in gold across the outside of the cup, only half-visible now: –*venter*.

Beside it is a sturdy white mug that looks almost completely undamaged by its time in the canal. Estimated to be from between 1925 and 1975, it, too, is made of porcelain, though it looks nothing like the translucent, gold-painted teacup.

Why were these cups thrown into the canals? Were they already broken? Or did people grow tired of them and throw them in whole? Were they tossed in after arguments or did they fall in by mistake?

Objects come and go from our lives. Some utilitarian objects can gather meaning as they persist, becoming more than the sum of their parts. Then again, what to one person is a treasured keepsake or an object of beauty might be somebody else's canal trash.

2

Sophie Moran, who is a production potter, thinks about a cup in terms of size, weight, shape, the look and feel of its surface, and how it sits in her hands when she holds it. Is the handle too thin – and at risk of breaking – or too thick? Can she fit her fingers in behind it? If yes, then how many: two or three?

Sophie makes functional tableware on the wheel. After deciding on a design, she works in collections, making the same piece again and again. Over the years, she became so skilled that her finished works started to look too perfect, like they were machine-manufactured.

'When I repeat something too often, I get good at it and then it doesn't look natural,' she says. 'I like it when it looks a little hesitant or tentative. Then they're a little different and have their own characteristics.'

Changing the clay she uses has helped her to resolve this issue. She gave up on porcelain's smooth perfect surfaces and now sticks to coarser stoneware, where each object shows the hand of the maker.

Cups are always popular, she tells me, because they're at an accessible price point. You can buy one, or two, or six. You can have a lot of mismatching cups in the cupboard and nobody will bat an eyelid, whereas with tableware, people tend to think in matching sets.

In her studio in Melbourne, she holds up two of her favourite cups of her own making. One has a white glaze, with a darker clay beneath. The other is dark brown, nearly black. They're both generously sized, with rounded forms and slim handles that can accommodate two fingers comfortably. The round shape formed by throwing the cup on the wheel has been altered by shallow carvings around the outside of the cups. They are sturdy, everyday designs, and unmistakeably handmade.

These are gorgeous pieces, but to Sophie they are also working prototypes – a visual reminder of the initial design of each range, so she can keep emulating the same piece. 'Each iteration of the cups is ever so slightly different because they are thrown on different days. The act of throwing is intensely of the moment. I might throw twenty to thirty of one form, and they capture the mood of the day.'

Sophie's work is heavily influenced by Japanese pottery, which she studied during her two-year diploma of ceramics. Years after first making contact with Japanese potter Akio Nukaga via Instagram, she visited him at his studio in Kasama, a city about an hour's drive from Tokyo.

She describes Nukaga's pottery as having a quiet, earthy beauty to it, with uniform shapes and straightforward forms – especially his cups – while his vases are often bulbous. His works are known for distinctive vertical lines called *shinogi* lines, a decorative technique where parallel grooves are carved into the surface. In the world of contemporary ceramics, he is one of Japan's most famous potters, and his pieces sell out quickly.

Sophie shows me a Nukaga cup that she bought before her trip to meet him. Afterwards, she realised it was probably made by an assistant in his busy studio. It is stoneware, made from red clay with a white glaze, in a simple cylindrical shape. It doesn't just sit on a shelf – it's her most used cup, from which she drinks her coffee, and sometimes green tea.

The Japanese philosopher Sōetsu Yanagi wrote in 1933 that *mingei* – or folk craft objects – must be made for daily use, and they must be ordinary things. They may be cheap, but they should also be sturdy. This perfectly describes Nukaga's cups.

A few years ago, Sophie spoke at an Australian Ceramics Association event, The Good Cup, as part of Sydney Craft Week. Potters crammed into a studio where Sophie shared stories about some of her favourite cups at the time (her favourites tend to change fairly often, as is probably true for many of us).

She interrupts her story to ask me what my own favourite cup is – at least for the moment. I mention a cup by London designers Edward Barber and Jay Osgerby for Royal Doulton, part of a forty-piece set called Olio. It is not a ceramicist's cup, but more of a design object, made in a factory in Staffordshire, and its plain form and neutral colours reflect that. Every time I use it, I am reminded of the designers themselves, whose British charm and infectious enthusiasm I have experienced in person when interviewing them for magazines.

Each potter who came along to Sophie's event also brought in a cup to swap, she tells me. They spent a few happy hours together talking about handles, proportions, clay bodies, heat properties, glazes: all the secrets to making a good cup. Cups were exchanged, perhaps new favourites were made.

For potters, cups are true companions. 'There's nothing better than having a cupboard full of friends,' Sophie says. 'Stories stick to cups, more than they stick to other objects. A bowl or a plate stays on the table, but you hold a cup.'

3

Two and a half thousand years ago, when the Greek philosopher Diogenes decided to live out his extreme vision of a simple life – and give away all of his possessions – the last item he discarded was his cup.

This was in ancient Athens, a city obsessed with wealth and power.

Diogenes believed that everybody should reject society's pressure to accumulate things, as only then would 'your soul be in a calm and cheerful state'.

He made his home in a large jar called a *pithos*, set up in the public marketplace, even though passers-by called him a dog. He begged in the streets, asking not for charity, but for 'what he was owed'. When asked what wine he liked to drink, he said, 'Everybody else's.'

He was also a kind of ancient performance artist. One of his stunts was to carry a lantern through the streets in the middle of the day, saying he was 'looking for an honest man' but couldn't find one.

His fame grew. Later, he was granted an audience with Alexander the Great, who, standing over him, said, 'Ask whatever you wish of me.'

Diogenes replied (sunning himself), 'Stand out of my light.'

We have no idea what Diogenes actually looked like, though paintings and etchings from the seventeenth and eighteenth centuries show various artists' imaginings of him – in his jar, or with his lantern. Nor do we know what the cup he discarded looked like. But we do know why he threw it away. He saw a boy drinking water from his hands and realised – so the story goes – that since nature had provided him with hands, he no longer needed a cup.

This story takes on a new significance in a twenty-first century world drowning in objects, where discarded cups, along with all other kinds of detritus, overflow in landfill and fill the oceans.

Where will all this striving for new stuff get us?

4

It's Sunday afternoon. I'm at a repair café in Sydney's northern suburbs, where repairers are working with the owners of broken things in small groups at tables dotted around a community hall.

I'm sitting with Glenda Hoy, who has long hair reaching almost to her waist. She comes here on the first Sunday of each month to repair broken ceramics. Opposite her is the owner of two broken blue ceramic objects. He is tall and energetic, but seems a little shy. Also with us is a young trainee, hair tied back, polite, inquisitive, here to learn the ropes.

We gaze at the man's dark blue objects, almost black in the centre. They might be cups or bowls, but I don't think they are functional. I don't really like them – to me, they look like dinosaur eggs cracked open by hatchlings. But I remind myself that taste is subjective.

Glenda is in full swing, talking as she works, showing us her materials – liquid nails, then wood filler – describing how it should feel, what to look for.

The trainee asks, 'Do you use your finger to apply wood filler to the cracks?'

'Yes, because that's quite dry and crumbly. I can remove the excess better,' Glenda says. 'See this jagged edge?' she asks, pulling out a long file. 'I'm just going to take that sharp edge off.'

She is all process and technique. As she continues to file, using the weight of her body to steady herself, I ask the owner, 'Is there a story behind these?'

'No. Well, there's not a great story. Normally I have some colourful story. I went to this shop, I saw them and I bought them right away.'

I'll admit I'm disappointed. We turn our attention back to the blue objects and to the repair.

Glenda gives us a little history: the repair café movement started in Holland in about 2009, and spread around the world from there. But as a ceramicist, she first started repairing her own broken cups forty years ago. Then, about two decades ago, she started working as an art conservator.

For her, volunteering like this is a way of giving back to her local community. This is important for Glenda, because she herself was supported by her community when she was a single mother with young children. All the repairers and helpers here are volunteers.

The owner of the blue objects tells us he has tried to get them repaired before, but couldn't find anyone willing to take them on. He had a go at fixing them himself, inadvertently making Glenda's job more difficult by using a glue that is water-repellent and hard to remove.

Glenda won't repair cups that are intended for use (not just decoration) because boiling water poured for tea or coffee can dissolve the glue. The cup can break again, spilling its hot contents and causing burns. She also stresses the dangers of making ceramics – how certain glazes are not food-safe, how a broken edge of glaze can cut the hand like glass. She talks about kiln workers in the Chinese porcelain capital of Jingdezhen who die young of respiratory diseases due to long-term exposure to silica dust. It is a city where people do not have the privilege of growing old.

Pulling out a tube of blue paint and one of black, Glenda says that mixing the right colour is the hardest part of a repair. She gently dabs her blue-tipped paintbrush across the surface of the objects as we chat, peering through her magnifying glasses. She is nearly done.

Now the owner of the blue objects raises his voice above the grinding sound of someone's scissors being sharpened at a table nearby.

'Actually, there is a story,' he says. 'I was with some friends.

They have a nine-year-old and a seven-year-old who were scootering. I challenged them to a race and hit a section of the pavement. I went straight down. I was on the ground, and I pushed in here . . .' He touched his elbow. 'And there was nothing there. The bone was gone.' He stands and shows us the scar. 'It was the day before I was moving house. I was in hospital getting surgery when the removalists came. I returned to my new home to discover [these cups] had been broken.'

Glenda reminds him, as he gently wraps his blue objects in an old towel, preparing to leave, that they are not water-safe: he must never drink from them. They will have to remain on his shelf, silent sentinels to be admired from afar.

5

I wake, check my phone. A shower, then breakfast. My bowl is blue-and-white striped. My cup has a painting by Central Desert artist Lily Sandover Kngwarreye on it, feathery black strokes on white.

I stack cups on trays, turn on the dishwasher.

Select my shoes – black sneakers made of ocean plastic – and straighten my hair at the ends where it tickles me (I need a haircut). I grab my green umbrella on the way out the door.

Today, I'm off to the museum to seek out archaeological cups.

I walk through Erskineville, wondering which buildings used to be warehouses. I know this place was once a hub of manufacturing. My husband's aunt worked down one of these streets in the 1950s, in the laboratory at Bradford Mill, making bedding.

It's a hot, rainy day. I run for the bus.

At the Chau Chak Wing Museum, I'm self-conscious because my wet shoes are squeaking. The guard's shoes squeak too.

I do a quick circuit of the ground floor and upstairs, where there are scientific instruments and bark paintings. No cups.

Two levels down and it is all ancient Greek amphora, jugs, busts and tablets. Wait, here's a cup – with a long handle? I google *kyathos*. It's not a cup, but a cup-shaped ladle.

Now we're in south Italy, in the first millennium. Here are two *rhytons*. Another quick phone check and I see that, yes, these are cups for drinking, despite not having a flat base on which to rest.

One of the cups' bases is shaped like a ram's head, the other like a griffin. They are grotesque and fascinating. What sort of person would have drunk from these? And were they for everyday use or only for ceremonies or display?

Downstairs again, and we're in the Middle East: Teleilat Ghassul in Jordan, between the years 4500 and 3900 BCE.

Among the artefacts is a collection of 'ceramic cultic objects'. The label says that 'cultic' means it has been excavated from a building 'identified as a cultic sanctuary or shrine'. These were excavated by teams from here at the University of Sydney, between 1975 and 1977.

There's a cup here. It's called a cornet cup: starting cylindrical and coming to a point at the base (cornet means cone-shaped). It is an earth-red colour and smooth, but by no means perfect. It's almost possible to imagine the hands that shaped this 6000 years ago. Faint lines, where the red fades, become brown, hint at a possible decorative element. It is quite small.

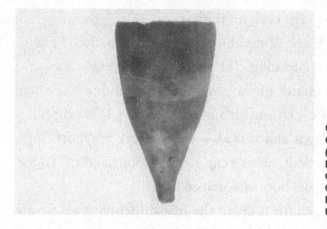

Cornet cup,
Chalcolithic period
(4500–3900BC),
NM78.173, Nicholson
Collection,
Chau Chak Wing
Museum, the
University of Sydney

As I look, I am conscious that a man close by is also examining these cabinets.

'Wow,' he exclaims, before he seems to realise that I am here.

After that, we do not make eye contact, but both stay quiet, stopping to look, read, then move on, stepping out the familiar museum choreography.

I like this museum. It's a mixed bag, but there's always something new to discover. In the café, over tea – plain white cup and saucer – and a sandwich, I look up Teleilat Ghassul and discover that the University of Sydney excavations there in the 1970s were led by an archaeologist named John Basil Hennessy.

The article says that Basil, as he was called, was 'well-known for his openness, warm nature and good humour'. He started his education late, after serving in World War II from the age of seventeen. His passion for archaeological digs was fuelled by his participation in a dig at Jericho in the 1950s, led by Dame Kathleen Kenyon.

This dig in the hot, dry desert proved that Jericho's Stone Age foundation was the oldest known continuously occupied human settlement. It made Dame Kenyon one of the most famous archae-ologists of all time.

Dame Kenyon herself was 'larger than life', according to one article. She grew up in a house next to the British Museum, which must have sparked her fascination for the past. She became the first female president of the Oxford Archaeological Society in an era when there weren't many women at university at all. She never married, and became one of the best-known British archaeologists of the twentieth century.

The rain is bucketing down when I leave the museum. I take shelter in the university library, a brutalist building. After a quick catalogue search, I'm on the eighth floor reading a well-worn book about Basil's excavations at Teleilat Ghassul, two decades after the Jericho dig. This is where the cornet cup I saw in the museum was dug up, about 20 kilometres from Jericho.

The book is almost impossible for a layperson to read – full of archaeological details, charts, numbers, jargon – and yet the warmth the authors felt for Basil is clear in the book's dedication, published after his death: 'For JBH'.

A photograph shows Basil with beard, glasses and polo shirt, crouching in the dig, walls of earth rising up on all sides. This is where Basil and his colleagues dug up this cornet cup, a small arte-fact that – along with many other ceramic shards – helped to prove the longevity of human settlement in this part of the world. Their hands were the first to touch this cup for 6000 years.

I sit by a long vertical window, alone on the eighth floor of the library, looking out onto a slice of rain-streaked roofs. Which of the cups that we hold and treasure today will end up being discovered in another 6000 years? Will anyone still be around to dig them up?

6

Kirsten Wehner grew up within the Mount Stromlo Observatory complex, on the top of a mountain near Canberra. Astronomical telescopes were housed in distinctive metal dome-shaped buildings around the bushland site, pointed at distant parts of the universe.

In the 1970s, when Kirsten lived there, families in which at least one parent was working at the observatory were given housing on-site. The astronomers and astrophysicists (mostly men at the time) would stay up all night making observations, and sleep during the day. They needed a quiet house. Their children would be sent out to roam the mountain.

Kirsten's father was not one of the men up all night. He was an engineer who worked during the day designing the telescopic instruments. When he arrived from Germany, he assembled his first telescope from pieces strewn across the floor.

In those days, teatime was sacred – everyone would drop what they were doing at the allocated hour and head straight to the tearoom. From when Kirsten was quite small, she was free to leave the house alone. She would walk through the pine forest to her father's office and tap on the window, and they would head to the tearoom together.

Milka, the tea lady, seemed to tower above little Kirsten. But Milka would always make a fuss of her, bringing Kirsten weak milky tea and biscuits, the two amusing each other as the only two females in a room full of male scientists discussing distant galaxies.

Now a curator at the National Museum of Australia, Kirsten embarked on a project in 2016 to record stories related to environmental crises. She discovered an object that deeply resonated with her own life experiences: a teacup from Mount Stromlo, fused in the extreme heat of the 2003 bushfires to a piece of aluminium from the observatory's telescopes.

Scorched teacup, a relic from the 2003 bush fire that destroyed the Mount Stromlo Observatory, National Museum of Australia

That firestorm razed Mount Stromlo Observatory. Everyone was evacuated in time and there was no loss of life, but the fire destroyed every telescope but one, melting their domes and shattering their glass lenses. When it was over, all the observatory buildings were gone, with only a shell of the administration building left. Books on shelves in the library had been reduced to columns of ash.

Many of the staff homes were also destroyed, but not Kirsten's childhood home. By then, Kirsten's father had retired and her parents had moved to 'town', to the western edge of Canberra. But they were not safe there either – their house was in the path of the fire.

In 2003, as the bushfire raged, Kirsten listened to the unfolding news from New York, while trying – and failing – to make contact with her parents. Eventually, she managed to reach her brother. Their parents were defending their house, he told her, but he'd had to leave them to protect his own home, also under threat.

When Kirsten returned home, she was struck most by what had happened to her parents' swimming pool. Within the blackened landscape of their garden, the pool's fibreglass surrounds had twisted and melted in the intense heat, but the water had protected the bottom and sides of the pool underneath: a blue opal of resistance.

The house, all its windows blasted in, had been saved by her parents using garden hoses. They had watched the houses on either side of them burn to the ground. One house had seemed to be all right, they told her, but then the bush next to the gas pipe had caught fire, and there'd been a big explosion.

Her mother already had some experience fighting fires at Mount Stromlo in 1952. That time, they had been able to beat back the flames and save the telescopes – though there was a lot less to destroy at the time. Back then, Kirsten's mother was working at Mount Stromlo as a researcher and was the only woman living in the 'bachelors' quarters'. Her father had been appointed but was still on his way from Germany – the pair met when he arrived later in 1952, and they married three years later.

When the catastrophic 2019–20 bushfires were burning across Australia's east, Kirsten's father, then in his mid-nineties, told her they reminded him of his experiences at the end of World War II. As a German soldier released from a prisoner of war camp in Scotland, he had slowly made the journey home across a devastated, blackened Europe, with smoke choking the air.

For Kirsten, the Mount Stromlo cup – ceramic fused with

molten metal – is an extraordinary object that evokes her childhood, where teatime meant safety and comfort, and the observatory's precious telescopes, tended to by her father, had not yet been melted by a firestorm. The violence of this fusing is why the observatory's telescopes are all now decommissioned; the site's value is historical more than astronomical these days.

How did that standard-issue office teacup get joined in this way to the aluminium from the telescopes? It must have been forgotten by a scientist working in one of the domed telescope buildings on the mountain's summit. Perhaps they took a cup of hot tea into the dome while they were working, to stay awake. The telescope searched for nebula – enormous clouds of gas and dust in outer space, the birthplace of stars – as the firestorm slowly gathered strength.

The astronomer sipped their tea, checked the clock, sighed. The long night hours stretched ahead.

7

An ordinary kitchen bench in an ordinary kitchen. A collection of washed dishes and pots are piled high on a red drying rack, plate upon upturned cup, more plates still, an upside-down bowl in blue and white, a utensil jutting out at an odd angle, a saucepan resting precariously on top. Beside them, on a stainless-steel drainer: a crumpled tea towel and a teacup and saucer filled with hot tea.

The painting, called *Washing Up*, is a wood block print by Australian artist Cressida Campbell. It captures something so banal, so workaday and unremarkable, that it instantly arrests me. It's a weekday afternoon. I'd like to linger, but I'm in a rush to catch the train back home to Sydney from Canberra.

The day before, staying with my parents in the apartment they recently downsized into, I mention I'm writing something about cups.

With that, all the cups start coming out.

Mum shows me two wide, shallow cups from Myanmar, made of a lightweight and flexible bamboo decorated in red on black lacquer. She bought them when she and Dad lived in Bangkok in the 1990s, from Elephant House, a shop owned by Myanmar-born Cherie, an acquaintance made through one of Dad's soil research colleagues.

Next, we peer through the glass doors of Mum's cabinet of best china – there are so many objects in there, each with its own story, that I can never keep track. But Mum knows the stories by heart – milestones, memories, treasures.

She points to a large teacup and saucer in exquisite porcelain, ornate gold and dark blue on white. This is one of those pieces that has been in Mum's family for generations. We don't know how old it is, except that it was old even when my grandmother was young. Mum turns over the cup, but there are no markings underneath to give us a clue.

A fine bone china tea set is carefully stacked on the shelf above: six cups, six saucers, six side plates, a jug and a large serving plate and bowl. These are also heirlooms, Mum says, probably from the same branch of the family, the Cormacks. They are less ornate but just as splendid, also in blue, gold and white. When Mum was a child in Brisbane in the 1950s, this was her mother's best tea set.

When her mother wheeled it out on her wooden tray mobile, Mum knew someone important was coming to visit, worthy of having their tea in 'the good things', plus a slice of my Gran's famous sponge cake with caramel icing.

Standing in the kitchen looking in the cupboards, where the everyday cups are, Mum hands me a robust mug in light blue and white, with her name (*Alison*) written on it. This was given to her by her aunt Gwen, whom her mother and everyone in the family said she was just like.

'Why?' I ask.

There was a resemblance, Mum says, but it was more than that. Their natures were similar. Gwen was never in a hurry, and she was creative, too.

On a higher shelf, I spot a mug I gave Dad when I was a kid. It says *I love Dad* in bright primary colours, with a picture of a house and the sun. Of course he kept it.

Last, Mum digs out a little enamel mug, beaten up, tiny, the size of a Japanese sake cup. This cup, she says, once hung on a hook above the stairs at my grandmother's childhood house in North Sydney, a lovely home with sprawling gardens. The day that my grandmother was tall enough to reach up and unhook the cup marked an important milestone when she was a little girl.

This is just like her, my gran. What was just an ordinary cup for water in the garden, she saw as a personal challenge. Her life was to change considerably in the coming decades, orphaned as the eldest of five children, surviving the Depression and the war, but never losing her sense of humour. Life was a challenge to be overcome. Even in her eighties, she was strong – I can still remember her iron grip when she held my hand.

8

Mr and Mrs WS Garrad
Kendall Dale
Milton NSW

25 January 1946

To my dear Mother and Father,

I hope this letter finds you well. Our trip home went well, with only three stops for supplies and petrol. The car fared well on the dirt road that had been so treacherous on the way over. Now the water from last month's rain is nearly gone it was much better. John says they will start building the extension to the Princes Highway soon now that the war is over and that will make things much easier to get home. He reckons the car trip from Milton to Coniston could take as little as three hours once they finish.

We took your advice and stopped in at Faust's Newsagency and Gift Store in Milton on the way and they had several lovely tea sets. I bought the matching sugar bowl and jug, which are white with a beautiful colour illustration of the main street in Milton, with the words 'The Princes Highway, Milton, N.S.W.' written underneath. In the shop, Hans said they are fine bone china, made by Royal Stafford China in England. The illustration is based on a photograph apparently.

I have unpacked them and put them in the china cabinet to remind me of you and home. It goes very well with the tea set I bought in Albury, and the other Royal Albert cups.

I do hope you can visit us some time during the year. Otherwise, we will visit again soon.

Your loving daughter,

Grace

Note: This fictional letter is based on information published on the Storyplace website about a real sugar bowl and jug in the collection of the Milton Ulladulla Historical Society.

9

As vessels made from clay, ceramic cups have an elemental quality to them. They connect us to the earth, grounding us. The empty space they hold can be interpreted symbolically; perhaps for this reason, they're used in rituals across the world.

On a cold night in Launceston, I was invited to take part in a ritual tens of thousands of years old.

A fire was put out, leaving red-hot coals. Eucalyptus branches were laid on top, producing clouds of smoke that stung our eyes. Mostly women, we huddled close against the wind and strained to hear, to learn.

Aunty Patsy Cameron AO held a cup in both her hands. The cup was simple, the colour of the earth. Inside was ochre mixed with water, a muddy soup warmer than the air.

She welcomed each of us in turn, painting a moon and two stars on the hand of every woman who came forward, using her fingers dipped in ochre. Her touch was gentle.

When we had all been painted, we talked, meeting new people, cradling our hands, still wet with the ochre. In that moment, I felt the strength of community and the power of ritual, like I had been let in on a secret, touched by Country.

10

Ladies

Make the tea, pour the tea, drink the tea.
Wash the cup, dry the cup, put the cup away.
Make the tea, pour the tea, drink the tea.
Wash the cup, dry the cup, put the cup away.

Only four poems by Chinese poet Bao Junhui still exist.
In one, she tastes tea at dawn.
After leaving the women's quarters of the palace, passing
   windows and blinds,
to the East Pavilion, where tea awaits.
Views of mountains, bamboo, hibiscus.
As music plays in gentle chords from below.

Ten centuries later, in Europe, and porcelain fever grips
   the upper classes.
Sailing ships laden with blue and white crockery; white
   gold.
Jane Austen writes to her sister Cassandra about the
   pleasure of receiving, unpacking and approving her new
   Wedgwood.

A handle is invented to stop ladies from burning their
    fingers.

Queensland. 1920s.
How to read tea leaves.
Are you looking closely?
What shapes can you see?
Do the leaves look shapeless?
Keep looking.
Maybe you are not a natural.
Make sure you use quality Bushells tea.

Meanwhile, in Paris,
after she wears a particularly fetching fur bracelet to lunch,
Picasso suggests that sculptor Méret Oppenheim cover
    everything in fur.
'Even this cup and saucer?' she laughs.
She is twenty-two and already the toast of town.

1982. Commonwealth Games. My gran has been to the
    souvenir shop.
The blue and red logo and mascot – Matilda the
    Kangaroo – on everything.
She decides to wear all of her purchases at once.
A hat with mini-umbrella fitted.
A scarf covered in red and blue logos.
Other souvenirs she hangs off her ears or holds – like
    the mug with Matilda on it – as she struts through the
    living room.

Do we still have that mug?
I hope so.

Caught the flu? Tea.
Failed your exam? Tea.
Death in the family? Tea.
Calamities calmed with milk and one sugar.

It's 2023 and Emily (@snackqueen666) is not crazy.
Her boyfriend's favourite mug, with his first initial on it,
   was not given to him by his ex.
When the pair moved in together, the *Daily Mail*
   explains, Emily had to 'deal with seeing the mug all
   around their home'.
But Emily finds out the truth at Christmas, when his
   stepdad gives her a mug with her first initial on it.
'That is so cute and I suddenly love this mug,' says Emily.
Crisis averted.

Boil the kettle, pour the tea, drink the tea,
Wash the mug, dry the mug, put the mug away.

The Extraordinary Edward: A Life Stripped Bare

Introduction by
Nick Feik

In conventional accounts of colonial Australian history, there is no room for a character such as Edward de Lacy Evans. Nor do common understandings of Victorian morality incorporate narratives of lives like his.

Sam Elkin's portrait, which reconstructs as much of Evans' life as sources allow, is a challenge to our perceptions of Australian history as well as being an act of creation. This is not to imply any fictional element or trickery; Elkin is simply looking for something that previous writers – with a few notable exceptions – have rarely sought. 'In the early stages of my own gender transition, I was hungry for evidence of my own kind,' Elkin recounts. He looked for, found, and then re-created something more than a historical character.

This essay clears a space in the Australian narrative for an identity largely ignored or excluded from settler histories. In reality, settler society did contain a space for gender-diverse people – however circumscribed and painful – and, as Elkin shows, Edward de Lacy Evans wasn't alone. He wasn't even unique to the goldfields in living as a man having been assigned female at birth.

It's Evans that Elkin keeps returning to, for fascinating and instructive reasons. Elkin reinscribes Evans into the world and makes it a richer place.

The life of Edward de Lacy Evans can't be reduced to truisms about 'life in the colony', because it was never straightforward, and the historical sources that remain contain ambiguities and biases that cannot be straightened out, even if that were the aim. Journalistic accounts of Evans' life were full of Victorian-era prejudice: reporters were scandalised, confused, sensationalised and, above all, thoroughly humiliating and disapproving. The few photographs of Evans present their own moral quandary. They were taken under duress, and represent a dark legacy of the time, in which difference was treated as medical freakery for the benefit of 'gawking onlookers'. Elkin is right to feel conflicted looking at them today, and to question whether they should be available for a new public to judge. He asks, do the photos offer the opportunity for 'people like me' to find themselves reflected in history? Does this 'make up for the hurt that they caused their subject? Is it important for these images to exist so that we can look squarely into Evans' haunted eyes to ensure that this never happens again?'

Yet Elkin, with his careful eye for detail and sensitive, intuitive reading of subtext, can see another side of this essentially sad tale. His perspective carries its own grace, but Elkin sees beyond the limits of the source material. With empathy and imagination, he presents possibilities that, while remaining unprovable, nevertheless now exist as possibilities.

He bestows a dignity to the life of Edward de Lacy Evans that cannot be unwritten.

The Extraordinary Edward: A Life Stripped Bare

Sam Elkin

IT'S THE PHOTOGRAPHS THAT HAUNT ME.

In the first image, Edward De Lacy Evans, a stately looking man with thick, wiry hair, stands for a portrait in his dark three-piece suit. He appears well nourished; the buttons of his waistcoat strain slightly. The sleeves of his suit jacket, on the other hand, billow at the elbow, an inch too long for his dimensions. His hand is placed proprietorially on the shoulder of a seated young woman in a pale, floor-length frilly dress. She looks to be no more than twenty. Her tight dark ringlets have been scraped back severely from her face, and her waist is cinched with a bow. In her right hand, she's holding a copy of an open book, which I assume to be the Bible. Unlike the man, her face is set in a grimace. But what exactly does her expression convey? Anger, fear, maybe defiance?

As I sit in a grand reading room at the State Library of Victoria, staring down at the small sepia print, I notice a blemish that interrupts the march of the border. Is it a tear stain? Drop of blood?

The second image appears to be a bust shot of a woman in a hospital bed. She looks pained and gloomy, with dark cavernous rings under her eyes. Her short wavy hair has been brushed neatly with a middle part, and she's wearing a white, rigid, high-necked shirt. Is that a tightly buttoned nineteenth-century hospital gown, or a straitjacket?

This too is Edward De Lacy Evans.

In the third image, the man is back, his face a little thinner. This time his suit is paired with a black bow tie. But who is that next to him? It's not the angry young woman from the first photograph, or the patient from the second, but an elegant lady dressed in a lavish, flowing ball gown, her hair piled high in a decorous bun. They could be brother and sister – twins even – as they stand together in a parlour. It is, in fact, a trick photograph: two full-length portraits of Edward De Lacy Evans, dressed in a long gown on the left and in a three-piece suit on the right.

I've been fascinated by Edward de Lacy Evans since I saw lesbian historian Julie Chesser present a lecture on him, based on her book, at a queer student conference at the University of Melbourne in 2008.[1]

Fifteen years later, I followed a Goldfields pride festival walking tour to reacquaint myself with his life. Thirty ageing history buffs

---

1   Chesser, Julie, *Parting with my Sex: Cross-Dressing, Inversion and Sexuality in Australian Cultural Life*, Sydney University Press, 2008.

congregated around a large rainbow umbrella outside an unremarkable brick building, the former home of the *Ballarat Courier*.
Mindful to keep out of the way of pedestrians, we bunched together
as an amateur historian recited the news story as it was broken by
the *Argus* on 3 September 1879:

> A curious incident has occurred at Kew Lunatic Asylum. A lunatic
> was brought from Sandhurst by the police, and was admitted
> into one of the male wards. The patient was tolerably quiet until
> preparations were made for giving 'him' the usual bath. On
> the attendants attempting to carry out the programme, violent
> resistance was made, the reason for which proved to be that the
> supposed man was in reality a woman. The most singular part
> of the affair is that the woman had been received into Sandhurst
> Hospital as a male patient and sent thence to the asylum under the
> name of Evans. She states that she has lived at Sandhurst for many
> years dressed in male attire. Her age is about 35.[2]

The historian paused briefly, unable to compete with the roaring
belch of a passing Harley-Davidson before reading out the *Bendigo
Advertiser*'s follow-up story:

> One of the most unparalleled impostures has been brought to light
> during the past few days, which it has ever been the province of
> the press of these colonies to chronicle, and we might even add is
> unprecedented in the annals of the whole world. A woman, under
> the name of Edward De Lacy Evans, has for 20 years passed for a

---

2   *The Argus*, 3 September 1879.

man in various parts of the colony of Victoria . . . As it is almost impossible to give an account of the case without making use of the masculine pronoun when referring to Evans, we propose to use that appellation . . .[3]

Evans was not the only person to be revealed as assigned female at birth after living as a man in colonial Victoria. Indeed, he wasn't even the only one in the goldfields. The very same year Evans was outed, Dr Henry Slade, a thick-moustached American spiritualist who toured his show through the Australian goldfields, was revealed to be female-bodied after falling ill on his homeward-bound steamship.[4] Edward 'Old Ned' Moate of Bright, a long-serving manservant to several prominent men, was also revealed to be female-bodied following his breakdown and institutionalisation in Beechworth Asylum.[5] Then there was Johann 'Jac' Jorgensen, a German-born farmhand and member of the Enmore Volunteer Mounted Rifles, whose gender history was revealed upon his death in a bush shack in 1893.[6]

There were plenty of pragmatic reasons for women to temporarily don a male disguise. The rudimentary, unlit country roads could be perilous for women, and it was deemed somewhat forgivable to journey in male attire in the interests of chastity. Indeed, *Philip's Emigrants Guide to Australia*, an 1855 guidebook popular with new arrivals, published several stories of young women arriving at the goldfields in male disguise. But the notion that a

3 *Bendigo Advertiser*, 4 September 1879.
4 'Dr. Slade the Spiritualist: A Woman', *The Capricornian*, 11 October 1879, p. 15.
5 'Peculiar Deception. A Woman Impersonates a Man', *Evening News* (Sydney), 25 July 1884, p. 2.
6 'The Elmore Male Impersonation Case', *Bendigo Advertiser*, 13 September 1893, p. 3.

woman might simply choose to live full-time as a man, despite evidence of many having done so, apparently remained unfathomable to the mainstream culture.

My journey into the archives began during the early stages of my own gender transition. I was hungry for evidence of my own kind, searching for proof that I hadn't been duped by a global fad that was killing off butch culture and stealing women's rights to single-sex spaces. I found others like me who had repudiated their womanhood. There was Scottish doctor Sir Ewan Forbes, whose family dispute over his right to inherit a baronetcy formed one of the most intriguing British legal gender stoushes of the twentieth century. I was moved by the records of southern gospel singer Willmer 'Little Axe' Broadnax, whose gender history wasn't revealed until after his death. I was also fascinated by North American itinerant hunter and bear tamer Joseph Lobdell, who was locked up in a New York asylum in 1879.

But it's Edward de Lacy Evans to whom I've always returned.

Evans travelled from Plymouth, United Kingdom, in 1856 aboard the *Ocean Monarch* bound for Melbourne; on the shipping list, he was registered as Ellen Tremayne. The 26-year-old Roman Catholic maid from Kilkenny could read and write, unusual for a working-class Irish woman at the time. Evans was later described as having been 'somewhat strange in her behaviour on board ship. She used to wear gentlemen's undergarments and tried to make the other girls believe she was a man.'[7] His trunk full of men's clothes,

---

7 'The De Lacy Evans' Case,' *Bendigo Advertiser*, 11 September 1879, p. 3.

mysteriously labelled as belonging to an 'Edward de Lacy Evans', was much remarked upon. Evans was said to be popular with the ladies; he was rumoured to have had at least two sexual relationships with women during the gruelling and perilous 188-day journey.

When the ship finally landed in Hobson's Bay, Evans spent a few days in Melbourne before trudging 40 kilometres north-west towards a hotel in Melton run by a publican named McKeddie, where Evans was to be employed as an indentured female domestic servant. In an era when signs emblazoned 'No Irish Need Apply' were strung up across the colony, prejudice narrowed in on Irish Catholic women from the rural south, who were vilified as slovenly, uncivilised and dim. Evans did not last there long. McKeddie asked Evans, who was still presenting in female attire, to sleep in a bed with Mrs McKeddie 'for company' while he was away on business. While female servants sleeping alongside their mistresses was not an uncommon practice in the era, a real or imagined sexual encounter seems to have occurred, as McKeddie horsewhipped Evans upon his return. Evans, no doubt frightened and traumatised, left his job and hastily trekked back to Melbourne.

He took up living as a man full-time and soon married Mary Delahunty, an independently wealthy Irish governess who had been a fellow passenger on the *Ocean Monarch*. Their union was solemnised at St Francis' Church on Lonsdale Street, Victoria's oldest Catholic church. Their 1856 marriage is now considered the first known queer Australian nuptial ceremony.

The couple moved 90 kilometres north-west to Blackwood on the Lerderderg River. Delahunty set up a school, while Evans found work as a miner. He just missed his chance to strike it lucky panning the creeks for nuggets of alluvial gold and was instead employed in one of the first quartz mining operations in the district, digging holes and excavating shafts to reach the harder-to-access crystalline gold. Quartz mining was notoriously labour intensive, and this must have been a challenging time for Evans as he adapted to his new life underground.

Delahunty and Evans' relationship ultimately didn't last. She went on to marry a prominent American mining surveyor, 'outing' Evans in the process by successfully arguing that her marriage to Evans was void on the grounds that Evans was biologically female. Delahunty settled in nearby Daylesford, while Evans took off for Bendigo (then known as Sandhurst) to begin a new life. There he reinvented himself as a widower and nephew to the British Army General de Lacy Evans, who was then a household name for his exploits in the Crimean War. Evans explained away his current straitened circumstances with a tall tale about a recent failed mining venture. While Evans' tale might today be taken as evidence of chronic duplicity, the ability for settler men and women to reinvent themselves was practically baked into the makeshift design of colonial Australian society.[8]

Evans soon remarried, this time to a young woman from Northern Ireland called Sarah Moore. They were wedded in a local Protestant church; it seems that Evans was officially done with Catholicism. The newlyweds celebrated their union at Billy Rodda's Golden Square Hotel, a large pub still standing in Bendigo today. Moore, at five foot ten, was said to have enjoyed a drink and towered over Evans, who was five foot five.

---

8 Bishop, Catherine, 'Women on the Move: Gender, Money-Making and Mobility in Mid-Nineteenth-Century Australasia', *History Australia*, 2014, 11:2, pp. 38–59.

Evans and Moore were employed by a farmer named Brennan in the nearby town of Emu Creek, who later described them as 'splendid, indomitable workers'.[9] Brennan recounted that Evans 'worked at ploughing, hay mowing, potato digging, blacksmithing, tree grubbing, and chaff cutting, and was a hard worker at all, and especially skilful at ploughing'.[10] Moore was said by Brennan to be a fairly 'masculine woman', while Evans came across as 'small and somewhat effeminate'.[11] For five years the hard-working couple lived and worked across the goldfields, until Sarah Moore died from tuberculosis in Eaglehawk after a two-year illness, aged just twenty-eight.

The next year, Evans married Julia Marquand, the stern-looking young woman in white whose photograph with Evans is preserved at the State Library of Victoria. On their marriage certificate, Evans described himself as a 28-year-old from Paris (he was in fact a decade older). While Julia Marquand was a humble French dressmaker's assistant, her older sister Louisa had married a wealthy and influential mining speculator, Jean Baptiste Loridan. Loridan helped Evans land a job in the New Chum Extended Company's quartz mining operations.

Quartz mining was a dirty, dangerous occupation, and around 1886 Evans suffered a serious head injury from a large piece of falling quartz. He was treated by a doctor and soon returned to work, but was said to have 'complained greatly of his head' in the coming years.[12] Marquand later reported that he had been 'laid

---

9 'The Man-Woman Evans', *Gippsland Times*, 10 September 1879, p. 4.
10 'Man Impersonators: Some Notable Cases,' *Canowindra Star* and *Eugowra News*, 14 October 1910, p. 6.
11 Ibid.
12 Interview with Mrs. Evans, *Bendigo Advertiser*, 4 September 1879, p. 2.

up in bed for two months with fever', and reportedly underwent a significant personality change following the accident: 'He continued to be very strange in his ways, and was very exacting in his requirements, and if everything was not ready for him and done to his liking he would "blow up fearful", and she was told by Dr J Boyd that he was not safe to be left alone.'[13] It's plausible Evans sustained a traumatic brain injury that contributed to his declining mental health.

The following year Marquand became pregnant and had a healthy baby daughter, Julia Mary. Due to his anatomy, we can safely assume that Evans was not the biological parent. While he accepted his role of father of Marquand's child, the couple later gave evidence that Loridan had repeatedly 'seduced' his sister-in-law between forty and fifty times while Evans was at work, resulting in the pregnancy.[14] While neither Marquand nor Evans directly described Loridan's behaviour as rape, their descriptions of the encounters do not read as consensual.[15] These assaults, along with the economic control Loridan exercised over the couple, would certainly have been significant factors in Evans' apparent breakdown.

On Friday 18 July 1879, Evans was sent home from work at the Great Southern mining company, on the grounds that 'there was something wrong with him'. Loridan, who was both a significant investor in the company and a board member of the Bendigo Hospital, brought Evans into the local ward to be treated for a

---

13 Ibid.
14 'The Maintenance Case', *Bendigo Advertiser*, 6 December 1879, p. 3.
15 Ibid.

'bodily illness'.[16] Evans refused to bathe, and fled to his home in Quarry Hill. He was arrested by police the next day and committed to the lunacy ward of Bendigo Hospital under the Lunacy Statute on the grounds of 'incipient softening of the brain'.[17] For his six-week stay, he again refused to bathe, and the staff did not insist. As he had not been declared cured of insanity, Evans was then transferred by a police constable to Kew Asylum.

Despite its elegant Italianate architecture and beautiful views of the Yarra River, Kew Asylum was a mess. Beset by overcrowding, mismanagement, lack of resources, poor sanitation and disease, it was also the scene of Evans' now infamous forced gender reveal. The Kew Asylum record noted that, upon admission, Evans 'resented any examination in the waiting room, and was taken to D Ward, where on undressing to take a warm bath it was found that "*he*" was a *woman*. What makes it more extraordinary is that she had been an inmate at the lunatic ward of the Bendigo Hospital where her sex had not been discovered.'[18]

News of a crossdressing miner in Kew Asylum was soon leaked to the newspapers, and a national scandal erupted. Over the coming weeks, local journalists sought interviews with anyone they could find to shed light upon Evans and how he'd managed to 'deceive' so many for so long. One of the few direct quotes purported to be from Evans was printed in a local newspaper about the incident: 'The fellers there took hold o' me to give me a bath, an' they stripped me to put me in the water, an' then they saw the mistake. One feller

---

16 'Further particulars', *Bendigo Advertiser*, 5 September 1879.
17 'An Extraordinary Case', *The McIvor Times* and *Roney Advertiser* (Victoria), 11 September 1879, p. 2.
18 Public Records Office of Victoria, VPRS 7397/P/1-5. Kew Asylum Case Books 1871–1912. Female Entry casebook no.5, entry 182, 1 September 1879.

ran off as if he was frightened; the others looked thunderstruck an' couldn't speak. I was handed over to the women, and they dressed me up in frocks and petticoats.'[19]

Evans was said to have taken these off and refused to get out of bed. He was then subjected to an invasive, non-consensual gynae-cological examination without sedation, the notes of which were published in a medical journal:

> The vaginal orifice was small, only just admitting the index finger, leading to a smooth walled vagina of natural capacity. The sound was introduced to the uterus after much difficulty, by introducing the left index finger into the rectum and guiding the instrument in . . . the ovaries were not made out specially, as the examination had already lasted some time, she was weeping and sobbing the whole time, but making no determined resistance.[20]

The doctor determined that Evans had previously given birth at least once, a fact that caused a further frenzy of media speculation about what had happened to the child. Evans was said to have confirmed this fact to the doctor who performed the examination: 'He asked her what reason she had for adopting the disguise . . . and her answer was that she didn't know, but that after she had the illegitimate child, she "went to the bad", and changed her name so that she would not be known.'[21]

The *Bendigo Advertiser* published a follow-up article,

---

19 *The History and Confession of Ellen Tremaye, Alias, De Lacy Evans, the Man-woman*, 1880, WM Marshall, p. 26.
20 Penfold, Oliver, 'The Case of Man-Personation by a Woman', *Australian Medical Journal*, 2(4) 1880, p. 147.
21 'The Man Impersonator', *Ballarat Star*, 12 September 1879, p. 3.

beginning with the claim that to 'give a circumstantial account of
the extraordinary vicissitudes of her career would fill the pages of
a three-volume novel, and we may safely add that the most fervid
imagination of writers of fiction fall short of the plain facts of this
strange story'. The 'shocking' additional revelation was that Evans
had taken a steamship prior to emigrating to Australia from Ireland
to Quebec, Canada, with the father of the child, where the infant
subsequently died.[22]

Evans was returned to Bendigo Hospital, where he went on a
hunger strike. Mrs Holt, the matron, who claimed to have been
a fellow passenger on the *Ocean Monarch*, described Evans as 'a
most determined woman . . . bent on starving herself to death'.
Providing further evidence of the medical violence that he was
subjected to, she disclosed that Evans had to be 'threatened with a
stomach pump before he agreed to drink some beef tea'.[23]

Evans received a visitor, likely his wife's brother-in-law Loridan.
Evans was said to have attacked him and attempted to steal his
clothes to escape. It was reported that Evans would have succeeded
but for the vigilance of Mrs Holt. In an egregious breach of patient
privacy, it was during this time that the photographer Nicholas
White somehow gained access into the lunacy ward to take pictures
of Evans. Perhaps through bribery or sheer exploitation, this is
the origin of the haunting images of Evans dressed in his hospital
shirt and the trick photograph of him dressed in male and female
clothing.[24]

---

22 'Extraordinary Case of Concealment of Sex', *Bendigo Advertiser*, 3 October 1879, p. 3.
23 'The Evans Personation Case', *The Armidale Express* and *New England General Advertiser*,
      19 September 1879, p. 3.
24 Colligan, Mimi, 'The Mysterious Edward/Ellen De Lacy Evans: The Picaresque in Real Life',
      La Trobe Journal, no 69, Autumn 2002.

Remarkably, just days after he was released from Bendigo Hospital, Evans gave evidence on behalf of his wife Julia Marquand in the Bendigo Police Court, who was suing Loridan for child support. It was during this maintenance case that Marquand disclosed Loridan had come to her house after Evans had left for work and 'seduced' her. He would enter the house to have sex with her at least twice a week, which he continued to do even after he knew she'd fallen pregnant.[25] Evans, who was clearly upset, was called upon to corroborate her story:

> 'Yes; I have seen him at my house. I don't want to go any further.' Then putting her hand to her sides, 'I am "hurted". Let me alone, sir, I have seen him.' The witness then looked at defendant, and said 'That is a fact: you are the father of the child, and here I am.' She then continued— 'I have seen him in bed. I cannot say anymore. There is influence; it is three years ago.' The witness then pointed to her breast, and said to the bench, 'It is hurting me here. I cannot speak it. That is all I can say, sir. The morning was fine when I saw Loridan in bed. I have seen him several times. I can prove I have seen him several times; prove it on oath before you all. I cannot say any more. I saw him many a time.'[26]

It makes for painful reading. To come to court at all after what he had been through seems an astounding act of courage, compounded by his having to do so in women's clothing, in full view of the reporters who had picked over his life, and a

---

25 'The Maintenance Case', *Bendigo Advertiser*, 6 December 1879, p. 3.
26 Ibid.

community who had only known him as male. As Lucy Chesser so eloquently put it, 'Few would have understood Evans' behaviour as courageous, or appreciated the irony that he almost certainly only submitted to this public humiliation out of a continued sense of responsibility for Marquand and her child.'[27]

Ultimately, Marquand and Evans' efforts were in vain. The claim was rejected, and Marquand and her infant daughter were left in poverty. Evans and Marquand never lived together again. After the loss of his own infant in Quebec, this second loss of a child must have been another devastating blow. In this regard, their story is a sad precursor to the long struggle for equal rights for rainbow families in Australia, which continues to this day.[28] Loridan soon wound up his business interests in Victoria and left for Queensland to invest in the sugarcane industry, while Marquand struggled on in Bendigo in poverty with a shattered reputation.[29]

Recently, the historian Robin Eames uncovered new material concerning Loridan, which casts him in an even darker light. Hospital records of another of Julia and Louisa's sisters, Fanny Marquand, reveal that this wasn't the first time that Loridan had had one of his in-laws committed. In 1878, just one year before Evans' own admission, Fanny Marquand was taken to Yarra Bend Asylum in 1878 by Loridan, where she was confined for thirty-five years, until her death in 1913.[30] Eames also discovered that fellow miners in Evans' workplace had been engaged in a long industrial

27 Chesser, Lucy, 'Transgender-Approximate, Lesbian-Like, and Genderqueer: writing about Edward De Lacy Evans', *Journal of Lesbian Studies*, 2009, 13:4, pp. 373–394.

28 lesbiansandthelaw.com/birth-certificates, accessed 9 March 2023.

29 Colligan, Mimi, 2002.

30 Eames, Robin, *The (extra)ordinary Edward de Lacy Evans*, Bendigo, 1856, 1879, Unpublished thesis, Chapter 1.

dispute against Loridan over unpaid wages, leading to the first miner's strike in Bendigo in September 1879, the same month Evans was admitted.[31]

Following his discharge, Evans had few choices for income other than to lean into his notoriety. In late December 1879, Evans reluctantly agreed to be paid to appear in travelling events by 'panorama showmen' Augustus Baker Pierce and William Bignell in Geelong and Stawell.[32] It seems, though, that Evans, no doubt deeply scarred by his experiences, was unable to play up to the crowd, and was soon cut from the production. Further commentary was published on what would become of Edward de Lacy Evans:

> And again the question arises what is to become of the woman. She is manifestly unfit for the hard work in mines to which she has been accustomed, even if she were permitted to adopt male attire en permanence, and she is quite unable to perform feminine work. Some good natured person might find her a valuable farmhand, and she might, at such employment, be able to earn a quiet living.[33]

Sadly, that kind-hearted person never materialised, and Evans left Bendigo for good. He appeared at the popular Melbourne Waxworks in 1880, also home to the death mask of the recently executed Ned Kelly. Evans was billed as 'The Wonderful Male Impersonator' and patrons were provided with a detailed pamphlet

---

31 Ibid.
32 Daily News, *Bendigo Advertiser*, 24 December 1879, p. 2.
33 Ibid.

titled 'The Man-Woman Mystery'.[34] He was then exhibited at 'Hiscock and Haymen's Mammoth Minstrels' at St Georges Hall in Bourke Street, and in a side show called the Egyptian Hall.[35] A sketch of Evans in a Sydney newspaper described him as follows:

> Her hands are large and brown, but very soft. They bear but few traces of the long years of rough labour she is said to have performed. Her voice is low, with a rough 'Geordie' inflection. Her figure, like a top-boot, is the same size all the way down, and she resembles a man dressed up in woman's clothes far more than a female clad in her proper habiliments. It is interesting to watch her, but not exciting.[36]

With reviews like this, it's unsurprising that the opportunities soon dried up. Without any other options left to earn a living in Victoria, and too old and traumatised to reinvent himself in another part of the colony, Evans appealed to be readmitted to the Kew Asylum. He was instead taken in as an inmate of the Immigrants' Aid Society's Home for Houseless and Destitute Persons, a series of ramshackle buildings on either side of St Kilda Road across from Princes Bridge (now the site of the Arts Centre precinct). Modelled on an English workhouse, the Immigrants Home provided a night shelter, convalescent hospital and long-term housing to single mothers, the disabled, and 'neglected' children.[37] Evans remained there for the rest of his life, known as Mrs de Lacy Evans.

---

34 *The History and confession of Ellen Tremaye, Alias, De Lacy Evans, the Man-woman*, 1880.
35 'Colonial Telegrams', *South Australian Chronicle* and *Weekly Mail*, 17 January 1880, p. 6; 'The Man-Woman at the Egyptian Hall', *Bulletin* (Sydney), 25 September 1880, p. 9.
36 'The Man-Woman at the Egyptian Hall', *Bulletin* (Sydney), 25 September 1880, p. 2.
37 findandconnect.gov.au/ref/vic/biogs/E000351b.htm, accessed 25 February 2023.

In 1896, a reporter, perhaps scratching around for a nostalgic news item in a quiet news week, sought out Evans, and provided this final character sketch:

> The masculine stride she acquired when wearing men's clothes is noticeable now. She smokes heavily also. Seated and dressed in feminine garb she does not strike one as a particularly masculine looking woman. She says she has a son, and that she was driven to leave home because her people did not like her marriage, and that she thought she would get work easier as a man. She has a nervous way of looking at newcomers, and when, after several furtive looks at me, she saw I was interested in her, sat looking at the floor. Her special work is to keep the matron's garden tidy – the work she prefers is digging.[38]

Evans died of the flu in 1901 at the age of seventy-one, a remarkably long life for the era. Upon his death, *The Argus* again recounted the facts of Evans' life, this time in reference to Murray H Hall, a New York politician who had just died and had been found to have a similar gender history. Every few decades thereafter, the story of Evans' life has been 'rediscovered' by journalists, a phenomenon that has continued into the twenty-first century: a series of takes that shine more light on the anxieties of their own era than of his.

In Evans' own lifetime and into the twentieth century, the recurring, salacious fascination of journalists centred on how he managed to deceive three women into believing he was biologically male. Just one example is the verbosely titled US newspaper article

---

38 'De Lacy Evans, the Woman Miner', *Daily Northern Argus*, 3 January 1896.

'The Queerest of Cranks: Astounding Story of an Individual Who for Twenty Years Figured as a Man, Married as Such, and the Secret of Whose Sex Remained Unsuspected Even, as is Claimed, By the Women Who Held the Alleged Relation of Wife.'[39] To me at least, the answer is obvious: of course his wives knew. Given the deep stigma against same-sex relations, it's unreasonable to imagine that any of them would have admitted to knowingly having sex with a woman. But Mary Delahunty, who travelled on the same ship to Australia, was most certainly aware. As for Sarah Moore and Julia Marquand, while it's possible they didn't know about Evans' gender history on their wedding days, it is an insult to their intelligence to think that they didn't soon find out. It seems that both chose to stay with him for as long as they could.

Interestingly, the newspaper reports sometimes describe a community in which Evans' birth sex appeared to be an open secret. One newspaper report wrote that many of Evans' mining co-workers had given him the nickname 'the old woman' – yet the same article concluded that 'nobody suspected the truth'. It seems that the obvious could not be stated: that people who lived outside the strict confines of Victorian morality were accepted, or at least tolerated, by most people in Bendigo. Indeed, Captain Moonlite (the moniker of gay bushranger Andrew George Scott) became a folk hero across the region. How many more were there like Edward De Lacy Evans and Captain Moonlite, whose queer lives never became grist for the journalistic mill?

39 'The Queerest of Cranks: Astounding Story of an Individual Who for Twenty Years Figured as a Man, Married as Such, and the Secret of Whose Sex Remained Unsuspected Even, as is Claimed, By the Women Who Held the Alleged Relation of Wife', New York, 29 November 1879, accessed via Nineteenth Century Crime and Policing: Monographs and Newspapers from the Library of Congress.

In the early twenty-first century, the revival of interest in Evans' life focused on its importance to the history of feminism and women's rights. In 2002, historian Mimi Colligan's formative article 'The Mysterious Edward/Ellen De Lacy Evans' (to whom she refers by birth name and with female pronouns), concludes that the 'sad life story . . . of Ellen Tremayne is an example of the lengths to which some women had to go in order to live as they wished'.[40]

More recently, Evans' life has begun to be discussed as a precursor to the modern transgender rights movement. Lucy Chesser's fascinating 2009 article 'Transgender-Approximate, Lesbian-Like, and Genderqueer: Writing about Edward De Lacy Evans' explores the story of Evans in this light, questioning whether it is truly possible to understand the gendered subjectivity of historical figures who did not record their own thoughts on the topic.[41] Traversing similar ground, albeit in a more populist tone, the *Sydney Morning Herald* in 2014 published an article by Olga Khazandec titled 'The Big Switch', with the opening precis 'An Irish Maid lived as a man in 19th-century Melbourne for decades. Was Ellen Tremaye Australia's first transgender person?[42]

While my own interest in Evans was first raised by seeing him as a cultural ancestor to my own existence in Australia as a transgender male, I don't believe that Evans neatly fits into any modern gender category in contemporary usage, whether it be transgender, non-binary or butch lesbian. None of these categories existed in his lifetime and, while tempting, it's entirely futile to

40 Colligan, Mimi, 2002.
41 Chesser, Lucy, 2009.
42 Khazandec, Olga, 'The Big Switch', *Sydney Morning Herald*, 16 August 2014.

guess what life choices the long dead would have made had they lived in our era.

In 2022, Bendigo Pride commissioned artist Chris Duffy to paint a mural of Edward De Lacy Evans in Chancery Lane in Bendigo to coincide with the region's annual Pride festival.[43] The image's stepping-off point is the trick photograph created by Nicholas White depicting Evans in both male and female attire. In the mural, however, Duffy has painted the 'male' Evans in full-colour and the 'female' Evans in black, as a kind of shadow of his former life. When I first saw this image, I must confess to feeling affronted; surely the last thing Edward De Lacy Evans would have wanted was a super-sized image of him dressed up as a woman adorning the streets of Bendigo. A local transgender rights advocate, Zara Jones, who consulted with Duffy on the creation of the work, explained her rationale for the design: 'There is this part of your life that has existed and that some people still see, within you. But it's a shadow. Your identity is forefront.'

The unveiling of the mural coincided with a formal apology from the *Bendigo Advertiser* for their historic news coverage about Evans. In an article titled 'This newspaper helped destroy life of trans man Edward de Lacy Evans', journalist Tom O'Callaghan wrote:

> Stripped naked in an asylum, against his will, Bendigo man Edward De Lacy Evans' life was about to become one humiliation

---

43 O'Callaghan, Tom, 'Bendigo Trailblazer de Lacy Evans Honoured with Chancery Lane Mural', *Bendigo Advertiser*, 15 March 2022.

after another . . . Now, 143 years after we published sensationalised stories about de Lacy Evans, it is time to acknowledge the
damage the *Advertiser* and other newspapers did. We helped
make his name a household one and, along with newspapers
across the world, fractured multiple lives because we cared
more about a story that interested the public, not what was
in the public's interest. It was wrong of this paper, and many
others, to describe de Lacy Evans as an 'imposter', a 'fraud' and
a 'criminal'.[44]

It's a moving apology, as late as it came. But what does it represent? Will something like this never happen to someone like Evans
again? Or will the tide turn again, and this apology be held up as
one of the worst examples of the 'woke' era of journalism?

In the end, I return to the photographs, despite how conflicted
I feel about them. These images, many of which were taken while
he was ostensibly under the care of medical staff in a locked ward,
are deeply problematic, part of a dark legacy of exploitative medico
freakshows and gawking onlookers staring at the mentally unwell
and those with disabilities. Should these original images, taken
under duress, even be publicly available via open access at the State
Library of Victoria? Does their potential value to people like me –
to find themselves reflected in history – make up for the hurt they
caused their subject? Is it important for these images to exist so that
we can look squarely into Evans' haunted eyes, to ensure that this
never happens again?

---

44 O'Callaghan, Tom, 'This Newspaper Helped Destroy Life of Trans Man Edward de Lacy Evans',
Bendigo Advertiser, 12 March 2022.

I have so many questions about Edward De Lacy Evans that neither these images nor the historical record can answer. What did he do for fun in Bendigo in the 1870s? What did he and Julia like to eat? Did his first child really die in Quebec, and if so, how? Did he know of any others like him on the diggings, who had crossed genders as well as the ocean?

Edward De Lacy Evans' life is most often spoken of as a tragedy, but to me he is a survivor, a jack of all trades who lived more lives than most, the best way he could for as long as he was able. He suffered setbacks, beatings, medical rape and the untimely death of a wife. Sometimes he played fast and loose with the truth, but who didn't in the fledgling colony? He was a participant in the dispossession of the Wadawurrung people, who'd lived on these gold-flecked lands for over 65,000 years. In just two centuries, Evans and his kind destroyed or significantly altered vital ecologies and life-giving waterways across the region, the effects of which are still being felt today. Evans was a traveller, an exile, and religiously flexible. He was also an early Australian workplace safety statistic. He was declared insane and then cured, declared a freak and then too boring to be a freak show. When he was called upon to do the right thing in the face of all who would humiliate him, he did it.

I like to think of Evans back in Bendigo before his accident, smoking a pipe and whistling an Irish ditty while putting down planks for his weatherboard house. His mind must've been filled that day with hope and wonder at just how far he'd come.

No One
Is Safe

Introduction by
Maddison Connaughton

In recent years, Australia has experienced a reckoning on consent. Landmark research, including the Australian Human Rights Commission's 2017 report on sexual assault and harassment on university campuses, brought to light the terrible extent of abuse faced by young people – finding nearly 7 per cent of university students were sexually assaulted the year prior, and more than 50 per cent were sexually harassed. In its wake, many universities moved to implement mandatory, evidence-based consent education. Similarly, the thousands of sexual assault disclosures from current and former Sydney high school students, prompted by Chanel Contos's campaigning, sent shockwaves across Australia. After tireless activism by survivors such as Saxon Mullins, New South Wales brought in affirmative consent laws, as did Victoria and the Australian Capital Territory. Many states have started teaching schoolkids a similar consent model – shifting away from the dated 'no means no' to ensure young people understand that only 'yes means yes'. In a little over five years, the progress, on paper, has been remarkable. But is it truly serving everyone in Australia equally?

The first time Wing Kuang and I met to discuss this story, it was over a coffee at a café in Sydney's inner west. We talked for so long, the owner had to kick us out to close – so we shifted to another café and kept talking. Wing's depth of knowledge on this subject, and commitment to investigate whether Australia's current approach to consent education was ignoring culturally and linguistically diverse communities, was so clear. She spoke about some of the young women she had already interviewed, who'd felt alienated by consent education clearly designed for White Australia with little thought for the country's cultural and language diversity. Of parents who were desperate to find in-language resources so they could help their kids understand consent, only to be told 'bad luck'. Of diverse community organisations bursting with advice for the federal government as it developed a new national curriculum for schools, which would include consent education – but the call from Canberra never came.

It's perhaps one of journalism's toughest challenges – making readers understand how badly formed policy can cause real harm in people's lives. Even the slightest whiff of politispeak will make eyes glaze over. But Wing has always spoken so clearly and powerfully about what is at stake here – in a society, no one is safe until everyone is safe. A consent education system that excludes culturally and linguistically diverse communities in Australia – a country where 22 per cent of people speak a language other than English at home, where almost 30 per cent of the population was born overseas – is one that will inevitably fail. Wing has done a huge amount of reporting to tell this story, alive to the nuance and complexity one needs when writing about subjects like race and sex. Her work is also extremely hopeful, showing that it's possible for Australia to build inclusive and effective consent education, if only policy-makers are willing to listen.

No One Is Safe

Wing Kuang

WHEN LILY READ THE HEADLINES ABOUT FORMER SYDNEY PRIVATE schoolgirl Chanel Contos on her phone in 2021, she was excited but also worried.

From the news, Lily learned that Contos – who was just a bit older than her – had discovered two of her friends had been sexually assaulted by boys they knew during high school, just as Contos was. Later, Contos launched a petition on her Instagram account to demand better, earlier sexual consent education in private schools. By March 2023, the petition had reached over 45,000 signatures.

Lily had also studied at a private high school in Sydney. But unlike Contos, she's an international student from China and joined the school's Year 10 class in 2015. When I first meet Lily in a café in Sydney's inner west, she has coloured her hair bright red, has a lip piercing and wears hot pants and a torn top with a Union Jack flag pattern. As she sits down in front of me, I think of my parents in China, who were unhappy for a few days after learning I got my first tattoo.

Despite her rebellious appearance, Lily describes herself as 'not a very brave person', but she still wants to share her story with me. 'I know every time someone speaks up, there will be people trying to humiliate them publicly, and that frightens me,' she says. She tells me she doesn't think her story can change anything, but she wants people to know what happens to young people like her when Australia fails to engage with culturally and linguistically diverse (CALD) communities in sexual consent education.

Like many Australian students, Lily first learned about the idea of sexual consent in her Health and Physical Education subject. Although the message she learned, 'No means no', had been criticised by failing to account for positive consent, it still left an indelible mark in Lily's mind. Two years later, when Lily began studying at university, she was mandated to take online consent training during orientation week. It was February 2018, when the MeToo movement was spreading from the United States to the rest of the world. Lily was inspired to explore the topic of consent outside the classroom. Her external reading, along with the consent training she'd done in Year 10, helped her to feel prepared to step into the world of dating and relationships – even in a country far from her family.

She began going on dates with a young man of her own age, but the sweet dating turned into a sexually abusive relationship.

Then endless sexual harassment from a male housemate began.

Then there was non-consensual intercourse during a make-out session with a male 'friend' in Sydney, even though, by that time,

New South Wales had enforced an affirmative consent law, which requires both parties to give a strong 'yes' before initiating any sexual activity.

Lily wasn't safe. She was taught about sexual consent at school, but it's very likely that these young men weren't. She was also worried about speaking up, because the perpetrators were from her own community – international students – and if she spoke up, she might be trolled or face revenge from people who shared the same cultural background as her. 'I don't think these guys actually know what consent is,' Lily says, followed by a long pause. 'Maybe it has come across them, but they don't really understand the concept, at least in an Australian context.'

Unlike Lily, who had access to sexual consent education at her private high school, her abusers only came to Australia for tertiary education. This means universities are the only places where these students might receive sexual education that addresses Australia's needs. Like the one Lily attended, several universities have launched mandatory online training for students, introduced zero-tolerance policies for sexual violence and developed mechanisms for reporting sexual assaults on campus. This was the result of the Australian Human Rights Commission (AHRC)'s landmark report about sexual violence on campus in 2017. The report was part of the $1.5 million Respect. Now. Always. initiative launched by Universities Australia, the peak body of the higher education sector, and it cited that 1.6 per cent of students were sexually assaulted in or around campuses in 2016.

But somehow, over the past six years, international students have been systematically excluded from this movement against sexual violence on campus.

In 2018, journalist Aela Callan launched her Al Jazeera documentary *Australia: Rape on Campus,* after noticing that the AHRC report had a very small pool of international students participating in the survey. During her investigation, she found there was a lack of culturally appropriate support for international students to seek help after experiencing sexual violence in Australia. In 2022, Universities Australia released their second report on sexual violence on campus. The figures were still shocking, as it showed one in six students had been sexually harassed in a university setting between 2020 and 2021. But this report was conducted during the pandemic, at a time when the majority of international students were not in Australia due to border closure, meaning that the situation of sexual violence against international students may still remain unclear.

Australia reopened its borders in December 2021, and international students have been making their way back. Within just January 2023, over 95,000 overseas students arrived in Australia. But even though students are returning to in-person learning, universities still seem reluctant to increase the number of resources for sexual consent education tailored to CALD students. In a report I did for ABC News in February 2023, I reached out to the universities of Group of Eight – the eight leading research universities in Australia – and asked about their policies on sexual consent education. While most of them planned to implement more measures to counter sexual violence, only one university, the University of Sydney, confirmed that they were developing multilingual materials on consent. In August 2023, at a senate inquiry into sexual consent laws, Universities Australia was questioned about its lack of transparency in running the Respect. Now. Always initiative that rolled out sexual consent education, while a small group of universities were reported to have rejected it following guidance from the sector's peak body. Senators also heard about the lack of culturally appropriate support from universities for non-Australian students who experienced sexual violence on campus.

I was a student reporter when the first AHRC report was released in 2017, and watched the development of consent education in universities closely. After I graduated, in 2020, I turned my attention to sexual education for school-age people in Victoria, and again I was shocked by the lack of resources for CALD communities. Even back in 2013, Ethnic Communities' Council of Victoria, one of the CALD peak bodies in the state, noted that there were 'significant service gaps, access issues and less optimal sexual health outcomes and experiences for many young people' in Victoria.

In March 2021, working for ABC News, I talked to Lauren French, a Chinese–Aboriginal Australian sexologist and senior educator at Melbourne-based Safety Body Australia. French told me her organisation had tried to apply for funding to translate consent educational materials into multiple languages, yet they got caught in the long process of grant application.

With campaigns like Teach Us Consent and young bright women like Grace Tame and Brittany Higgins speaking up about their experiences, things have started to change. In 2021, Victoria became the first state in the country to mandate consent education in schools. Speaking to me excitedly over Zoom in December 2022, French told me her organisation had received funding to deliver workshops on respectful relationships and sexual consent at language schools for newly arrived migrants, and there are a few more projects tailored to CALD communities on the way.

But these new resources for CALD communities only came after the mainstream group of students – who are not from CALD backgrounds – had their needs met. 'I think sometimes CALD communities can be the afterthought,' said French. 'Or the "Okay, we'll do it after we do this other thing", which I think is a real detriment, not only to all communities, but to this idea [CALD communities] would be missed.'

She acknowledged that Victoria's education mandate had built the foundation that enabled them to offer consent education resources for CALD communities today. 'So I think it just means that Victoria is just that little bit ahead of some of the other states, simply because it's just had more time to sit with it.'

But can modern Australia really afford to treat CALD communities as an afterthought when it comes to sexual education? To find out the answer, I boarded a train to Bankstown, a suburb located in Sydney's south-west.

As the train leaves Central Station, I watch the dramatic demographic change among the passengers inside the carriage. Initially dominated by white passengers, the carriage gradually fills with people of colour, from Middle Eastern teenagers to Asian workers in office outfits. It's a Monday morning in December, and after I get off the train, I follow a middle-aged Muslim woman wearing a brown hijab and nurse-like uniform through the exit, just one of a diverse group leaving the station with me.

Bankstown is part of South Western Sydney, one of the most multicultural regions in Australia, and has one of the youngest populations. The latest census data shows that six in ten people residing in Bankstown have parents born overseas. Its median age is thirty-six years old, with 19.3 per cent of its population school aged, between five and nineteen years old. These factors make Bankstown a crystal ball that shows what Australia will look like in the next five years. The census data shows 48.2 per cent of Australians have a parent born overseas, and over a quarter of the population were born overseas. The baby boomers, born between 1946 and 1964, have been replaced by millennials, born between 1981 and 1995, as the dominant group of the Australian population.

This swirl of statistics is why Oliver White, a 22-year-old university student and youth project officer at the National Association for Prevention of Child Abuse and Neglect (NAPCAN), also hopped on the train to Bankstown today. He is here to join a NAPCAN-run workshop about how to make the organisation's flagship respectful relationship education program, Love Bites, more accessible to CALD communities. Besides White, there are another twenty-five experienced sexual consent educators from NGO, schools and New South Wales government departments joining the workshop to share their experiences and insights of respectful relationship education.

First developed on New South Wales' mid-north coast in 2004, Love Bites is a practice-led initiative that offers interactive, conversation-based sexual education sessions for school students aged eleven to seventeen. It focuses on improving young people's understanding of relationship violence and equipping them with skills to explore respectful relationships. So far, the program has been delivered to over 10,000 students in New South Wales and has trained more than 4000 facilitators to deliver the workshops. In 2018, the Love Bites team began to collaborate with schools in South Western Sydney to deliver workshops, but the Covid-19 pandemic disrupted its progress. Now, as students return to in-person learning, the team has decided to continue its project, and this workshop in Bankstown is the first step.

Sitting in the corner of a conference room, White works as the facilitator, clicking through slides on his laptop as the speakers move between topics. During the break, he quietly joins a discussion among three attendants, listening carefully. White is a tall, thin young man who politely shakes my hand, a shy smile on his face. He grew up in regional New South Wales and later attended a private boys' high school in North Sydney. When the news about Contos's Teach Us Consent campaign appeared in headlines, he chatted about it with his female family members and friends, shocked to learn that they had had similar experiences.

'It provokes me to know that I need to be an ally, but not just a private ally,' says White in a Zoom call with me. He speaks slowly, calm but firm. 'Also, just going to a private boys' school, you do just see the ingrained toxic masculinity that breeds and festers within there that ultimately leads to some detrimental and harmful behaviours.'

But White's involvement with sexual consent education goes beyond private schools. At NAPCAN, White works with a group of young people – many of them with CALD backgrounds – to advise on educational programs for young people. He has noticed how race has invisibly shaped different experiences for him and his peers when it comes to dating and relationships. One of his close friends, a Muslim woman, shared the common debate about whether Muslim girls can kiss men before their relationships are 'sealed'. He's also had a conversation with his Nepalese colleagues at the pharmacy he works at on weekends about how to plan a date. They told White that men can decide many details of the dates, from whether to drink alcohol to whether their female partners can paint their nails.

These discussions prompted White to think further about what kind of consent education is needed in today's Australia. 'It's essential to be offering consent and relationship education in a variety of cultural and language forms,' White said. 'Western society has a tendency to assume that others can simply fit into our mould, and this just isn't true. Young people should be offered choices that they can access consent education in a culturally safe and relevant way.'

What is a culturally safe sexual education? Dr Brenda Dobia, a senior researcher and consultant for Love Bites, believes one way to achieve it is to embed the international human rights framework into sexual consent education. The term 'human rights' isn't just about political concepts like preventing violence, she says, but also about a universal goal that many humans, whatever their background, want to achieve. 'The bottom line with all of these is that we want positive relationships; we want that if we're in an intimate relationship, we want to get our needs met.'

Dr Dobia has been researching sexual education for First Nations and marginalised young people for the past two decades. 'If we talk about cultural diversity, you've got to know where you stand, and where others stand,' Dr Dobia tells me. 'It's about how we understand people across differences, how we understand the different life experiences, and how we make space for those voices, and not assume you know [about them].'

This is when Dr Dobia turns the discussion to a word that stigmatises CALD communities in the space of sexual consent education: stereotype.

It's not just gender stereotypes that young people of colour have to counter, says Dr Dobia, but also their cultural and racial backgrounds. And these stereotypes can become a barrier for young people with CALD backgrounds to access comprehensive sexual education, because authorities – such as schoolteachers – may opt not to deliver certain content to them, as they assume sex could be too sensitive in the students' culture. 'What you need to do for young people to get the skills they need is to break some of that down and go chat with them: "Where are you in need? What kind of relationship do you want?"'

Another person constantly frustrated by this stereotype of CALD communities is Nemat Kharboutli, the Strategic Support Manager at Muslim Women Australia (MWA), also based in South Western Sydney. Established in 1983, MWA has been providing domestic and family violence services, while developing several programs to empower young Muslim women.

When I chat with Kharboutli over Zoom in December 2022, it is the school holidays. Speaking to me from her home office, Kharboutli has to pause our conversation once to answer questions from one of her children. Despite her busy work and family schedules, Kharboutli is full of energy when explaining the work she's done for MWA. She's been involved with the organisation since she was a child, as a member of their youth camp. After graduating from university and working in several jobs, she joined MWA and devoted herself to the prevention of domestic violence within Muslim communities.

Throughout the years, she's heard many stereotypes and stigmas about Muslim communities when it comes to sexual education, from Muslim communities being conservative to the assumption that Muslim parents will not participate in sexual education because sex is a taboo in their culture. 'There is probably a different level of openness externally to have that conversation, because it's such a personal thing,' says Kharboutli. 'But the conversations are happening with parents and their children.'

At MWA, Kharboutli and her team developed several programs and workshops about respectful relationships, and they make sure the content is tailored to Muslim communities in Australia. One of the most successful programs MWA has run is Saving Face, a program dedicated to Muslim men and boys developed in line with other national domestic violence prevention networks. Through the program, Muslim men learn about respectful relationships and how to actively prevent violence against women and children, while discussing ideas such as masculinity, dependence and control with their peers and facilitators.

When MWA designs its programs, its first step is to form a team consisting of a theologian, a project coordinator and a researcher who bring together different perspectives of research and evidence about respectful relationships and domestic violence prevention. Then they run several sessions in which they invite people from the communities to take part in designing the content. 'Then we test it, go back, deliver it, and test it again,' said Kharboutli.

Besides these consultation sessions, the team also runs several surveys to better understand Muslim boys' and men's attitudes towards domestic violence and relationships, and some of the findings are surprising. One survey shows that, compared to

Australia-born young Muslim men, some men from older genera-tions actually have much more liberal mindsets around these types of issues. This finding contrasted with what Kharboutli's team had assumed and prompted them to revise the content accordingly and put it in trial again before rolling out the program nationally.

This approach of getting different stakeholders from commu-nities – especially young people – involved in the design of sexual education is called a 'co-design process', and it's been widely adopted in successful sexual education programs around the world. In 2019, criminal lawyer Katrina Marson used her Churchill Fellowship to conduct research about how sexual consent education works in Europe. She found that by getting young people involved in this co-design process, several schools and communities in Europe succeeded in making consent education up to date and relevant for its recipients. She also notes that different communities have different lived experiences, and co-design processes can help young people feel safe to discuss sex.

Marson's discoveries about co-design are also reflected in the overwhelmingly positive feedback from the Muslim communities towards the Saving Face program. In a response survey, all of the participants said there was 'significant or very significant improve-ment' in their understanding of Islamic principles relating to family and domestic violence, with 95 per cent saying they could now influence others to prevent family and domestic violence. 'We had the majority of participants say they felt like they were really able to articulate their thoughts around the issues, to express them with better language, and also had an improved sense of wellbeing when engaging in that conversation,' Kharboutli said. 'We do that by understanding the difference between culture and faith and where they intersect, because sometimes we just lump it all in together. And sometimes that's not accurate.'

Kharboutli also emphasises the diversity within the Muslim community – under the banner of Islam, there are over 172 different ethnic groups. There are also geographical differences within the Australian Muslim groups. An example Kharboutli gives is that in the Northern Territory, the Muslim population tends to be newly arrived skilled migrants, while Victoria and Western Australia have a large proportion of young Muslims. For Kharboutli, this means that even if the Saving Face program is tailored to men with Islamic faith, there are nuances that need to be addressed, not just culturally but socio-economically.

Basim Al-Ansari is another Muslim community leader from South Western Sydney who is passionate about young people's well-being, especially when it comes to sex and consent education. He is a healthcare executive and the son of Australia's most important Shiite religious figure, Ayatollah Mohammad Hussein Al-Ansari. But today, sitting in front of me in a black suit, Al-Ansari speaks as a concerned father of three young children, one girl and two boys.

Al-Ansari tells me that sex education has become a common topic among Muslim fathers during their weekly post-mosque catch-ups. 'Nowadays it's so easy to access porn on the internet, and we are talking that if we are not the ones who teach our kids about sex, then it will be the internet and porn that they learn about sex from.'

In Al-Ansari's opinion, what concerns Muslim parents about sexual consent education can be summarised in three questions: when is it the appropriate stage for the lessons, who will be teaching them, and what will they be taught? 'In fact, it is an individual issue for every parent that even the two parents of the same household may have different approaches towards it. Hence the various communities' voices need to be heard and involved.'

However, having sat in several advisory groups for different levels of governments for multicultural affairs, Al-Ansari worries that even though communities want to be involved, the governments and educational authorities may just forget to engage with them. 'What most of the government does is inform. It's not a rigorous engagement,' he said. '[Getting communities involved] doesn't mean having an information session to tell them, "This is the way we gonna do it, and you guys have to tell your community" – that's not what involvement should be.' He worries if communities aren't engaged in this process, some parents may refuse to let their children follow the curriculum.

And the design of the new sexual education curriculum – which the public had cheered for due to its incorporation of mandatory consent education back in 2022 – exactly reflects Al-Ansari's worry about governments' failure to engage with CALD communities.

In April 2022, federal, state and territory education ministers formally endorsed the latest version of Australian school education curriculum, also known as Australian Curriculum 9.0. In this new version, consent education becomes mandatory from foundation to Year 10, under the subject of Health and Physical Education. Another landmark for this new curriculum is that it is the first one that invited the Australian public to engage in its content design. The ten-week public consultation began in April 2021, around one month after Chanel Contos's Teach Us Consent campaign was launched.

Despite the public engagement, few people from CALD communities were involved with the consultation for Health and

Physical Education. In a report from the consultation organiser, the Australian Curriculum, Assessment and Reporting Authority (ACARA), there were 234 online survey responses, 321 email submissions and nine pieces of jurisdiction feedback received for the subject. The report also showcased a list of 232 organisations that emailed their submissions. Among them, only two organisations identified themselves as Aboriginal-related groups, and five groups identified themselves as CALD-related. There were no Islamic-identified groups listed in the report, but there were responses from six Catholic bodies and three Christian groups.

I asked ACARA how they decided which CALD groups to reach out to and engage with. In an email response, ACARA said they did not 'target any specific groups for their input into the consultation', as it was 'an open public consultation'. They also noted that individuals or groups who gave feedback via the online survey would be marked as anonymous, as well as individuals who emailed submissions, so it's possible that there had been input from CALD communities that were not listed in the report.

Neither Kharboutli nor Al-Ansari were aware of the curriculum consultation. 'In addition to the public consultation, we would welcome targeted consultations – using a combination of written and verbal formats – with multicultural and faith-based organisations, Islamic school associations and peak bodies, to create equitable access and trusted spaces for engagement on mandatory and optional syllabus components to strengthen co-design and cultural responsiveness,' Kharboutli said in an email to me.

Although the question about its engagement with CALD communities remains, the Health and Physical Education subject in Australian Curriculum 9.0 does appear to be more culturally and racially inclusive. In terms of developing students' understanding of multiculturalism, it has removed content about students participating in tokenistic cultural activities, but refined and added content about developing skills of promoting inclusion in their communities. It also highlights the intersectionality between sex and race. For instance, Year 7 and 8 students are required to not only 'examine the roles of respect, empathy, power and coercion in developing respectful relationships', but also 'propose actions they can take to promote inclusion in their communities'.

But there's another tricky issue. Although Australian Curriculum 9.0 has been endorsed by states and territories, it's still up to individual education departments to decide how much of the curriculum they will implement. For instance, Tasmania, Queensland and the Northern Territory all adopted Australian Curriculum 9.0, but they have taken different approaches to rolling out the sexual education aspects, especially within schools that have a large number of CALD students. Queensland hired eight curriculum officers to oversee the process, while the Northern Territory said they would work with educators like Love Bites to deliver sex education to CALD students. Tasmania said it would introduce its own sex education package based on the curriculum. There are also states that decided to roll out the new curriculum at a different pace. For instance, in January 2023, New South Wales said it would stick with the NSW Personal Development, Health and Physical Education subject, which activist Chanel Contos criticised as 'outdated'.

And while the mandatory consent training has been viewed as a milestone for Australia's sex education, more efforts are needed to ensure CALD communities can enjoy the benefits of the curriculum change. Sarah Lorrimar is from the Sexual and Reproductive Health Promotion team at Melbourne-based GenWest, which offers sex education workshops to newly arrived migrants and refugees. She's noticed that despite Victoria being the first state to mandate consent training, the time and resources needed to tailor comprehensive consent education are still lacking.

Lorrimar worries that without further resources, consent training mandated with only good intentions will end up being a checkbox exercise. For schools, it could become a situation in which holding one workshop that includes all the talking points from the curriculum is considered enough, when comprehensive sex education actually requires multiple sessions, and not only just in the classroom, but also outside of school hours. 'There isn't adequate time or conversation to create a safe space and actually unpack what sexuality education means to young people in the context of different cultures or language, people's own personal values and beliefs, and even their understanding of themselves,' said Lorrimar. 'You can't just come into a class and be like, "Hey, we're talking about sex today." It takes time to establish trust, to build comfort and to create spaces where young people can think about consent in the context of their own lives.'

As a former international student, I'm surprised by how governments and authorities have failed to engage with CALD communities. Before I came to Australia, I had learned that Australia is a nation known for its multiculturalism. How could this be the case? I turned to Sukhmani Khorana, a Scientia Associate Professor at the University of New South Wales. She told me that despite being multicultural, Australia has been pretending not to see the elephant in the room: race.

Compared to countries like the United States and Canada, which also have a large population of migrants, Australia is the only one that uses the term 'CALD'. 'If you use terms like "culturally and linguistically diverse" to understand people who are racially different, you are already hiding the fact that they're racially different,' said Professor Khorana. The idea of CALD was also reflected in the previous censuses by the Australian Bureau of Statistics, in which country of birth and language spoken at home were the main data collected as diversity indicators. While these two sets of data could be enough to understand the demographics of first-generation migrants, they are inadequate to capture the diversity of their children and descendants. Their children will be of the same race or ethnicity as them, but they will be born in Australia, and possibly speak English at home.

In June 2022, Immigration Minister Andrew Giles admitted that the failure of Australia to collect data on race and ethnicity had significantly affected Australia's 'understanding of different population groups', which he believed had created bigger issues during the pandemic, especially when it came to vaccination rollout. Later that year, the Australian Bureau of Statistics confirmed there could be changes to its approach to data around ethnic identity in the next census, scheduled for 2026.

Professor Khorana also noted that over the decades, government attitudes towards multiculturalism in Australia have not been consistent, and even the federal department that oversees multicultural affairs has its name changed frequently. 'It was [Department of] Multicultural Affairs at one point, then during the Howard years, they changed it to [Department of] Citizenship, so the focus is very much on "integrate or assimilate",' she says, adding that the ongoing lack of representation inside public service and parliament make it even more challenging for policies to reflect the lived experience of CALD communities, who are now in fact nearly half the population of the nation. In August 2023, the public servants' union, the Community and Public Sector Union, released its survey result of 173 public servants with CALD backgrounds. Only 33.5 per cent of them 'strongly agree' that their CALD background, connections with CALD communities and multilingual skills are recognised at work. Some respondents who work in CALD-focused positions noted that they found it difficult to access resources and training to make career progress, and some noted that CALD staff are rarely consulted in meetings.

I wanted to know what the federal government thinks about engaging CALD communities, especially with regard to sexual violence prevention, so I reached out to Education Minister Jason Clare and Immigration Minister Andrew Giles. While both men are Caucasian, they have publicly expressed support for Australia's multiculturalism. Minister Clare is the MP for Blaxland, which includes Bankstown, and he has spoken proudly of his public school education in one of Sydney's most multicultural suburbs. Minister Giles launched a review into the country's multicultural policies, which allowed CALD communities to make submissions in languages other than English. However, when Minister Giles first announced the review in February, he was criticised for not making it more visible to CALD communities. In February 2023, I requested interviews with both Minister Clare and Minister Giles. After almost two weeks, the offices of both ministers declined, but Minister Giles's office offered to give me a written statement. I sent three questions. One is about whether Mr Giles would consider dropping the term 'CALD' but use terms that more directly address racial diversity as a reference and parameter for governments – experts and demographers argue that the use of 'CALD' is failing to address the real challenges Australia faces in relation to multicultural society. I also asked for his response about the one-way consultations with CALD communities. I waited another week before following up. His media team said they would give me the statement within a week, but I never heard back.

In May, the federal government announced $3.5 million of funding directly for Chanel Contos's Teach Us Consent, while Minister Clare introduced an expert group to boost Respectful Relationship Education (RRE), which in some states forms part of Health and Physical Education at school. The eight selected experts, including Chanel Contos and Katrina Marson, are all well-known advocates for consent education, and some have been working for women's rights and sexual violence prevention for decades. Among the group members, Professor Peter Buskin and Dr NJ Newton are known for their research on engaging with First Nations communities and stopping sexual violence against Aboriginal children.

A spokesperson at the Department of Education told me the federal government will provide $77.6 million to states, territories and non-government school sectors as part of the National RRE Expert Working Group. She says that since the working group was launched in May 2023, the experts have been working on a rapid review into current RRE in schools, a Monash University–led respectful relationships education framework, and the design of the grants program. 'This includes providing advice on the delivery of RRE to priority groups, including First Nations people, people with disability, and CALD cohorts,' she says. 'Membership of the

National Respectful Relationships Education Expert Working Group was carefully considered to represent schooling sectors and expert members with a breadth of experience across RRE, including priority cohort groups.' She also mentioned that Monash University's RRE framework will incorporate CALD and other priority groups, and the following stakeholder consultations for the framework will invite educators and professionals who support the delivery of RRE to CALD students.

Four months after our first interview, Lily and I meet in a pub in Sydney's inner west, as I want to see how she is going. 'How about your dating life? Did you see boys?' I ask.

She giggles, telling me she is seeing someone. It is the first time since the end of her abusive relationship, two years ago, that she's gone back to serious dating, and she decided to follow her own advice to me: to take her time and know more about the person before deciding whether she would invest further.

My mind flies back to four months ago, when I asked Lily what she wanted to see from future sexual consent education. 'I want it to be delivered earlier. I want it to engage with everyone,' Lily had replied, determined.

We both look out of the pub, watching pedestrians walking past, with the sun sliding down to the end of the road. No one is safe until everyone is safe.

Bibliography

FitzSimons, Peter, 'What Chanel Contos Uncovered about School-age Sex Abuse, We All Need to Know', *Sydney Morning Herald*, 21 August 2022.

Friedman, Jaclyn and Valenti, Jessica (eds), *Yes Means Yes: visions of female sexual power and a world without rape*, Perseus Book Group, New York, 2009.

'Change the Course: National Report on Sexual Assault and Sexual Harassment at Australian Universities (2017)', Australian Human Rights Commission, 1 August 2017.

'Report on the Prevalence of Sexual Harassment and Sexual Assault among University Students in 2021', National Student Safety Survey, 23 March 2022.

Callan, Aela, 'Afraid, Ashamed and Alone: raped while studying in Australia', Al Jazeera English, 30 April 2018.

'Investigating sexual assault on campus with journalist Aela Callan', *Meld* Magazine, 15 August 2018.

'International Students on the Way Back', Universities Australia, 29 March 2023.

Kuang, Wing, 'Universities step up consent training', ABC News, 3 March 2023.

'Sexual Health, Cultural Diversity and Young People: what do we know?", Ethnic Communities' Council of Victoria, 2013.

Kuang, Wing and Yang, Samuel, 'Migrant parents call for support in sexual consent education as student-led petition gains momentum', ABC News, 18 March 2021.

'Canterbury-Bankstown: 2021 Census All Person QuickStats', Australian Bureau of Statistics, viewed 3 April 2023, https://abs.gov.au/census/find-census-data/quickstats/2021/LGA11570.

Martin, Peter, 'Australians are More Millennial, Multilingual and Less Religious: what the census reveals', *The Conversation*, 28 June 2022.

'Love Bites', National Association for Prevention of Child Abuse and Neglect, viewed 3 April 2023, https://www.napcan.org.au/Programs/love-bites/.

'Love Bites Canterbury-Bankstown', City of Canterbury-Bankstown, viewed 3 April 2023, https://www.cbcity.nsw.gov.au/community/community-services/young-people/love-bites-canterbury-bankstown.

Marson, Katrina, *Legitimate Sexpectations: the power of sex-ed*, Scribe, 2022.

'Final report: Health and Physical Education', Australian Curriculum and Assessment and Reporting Authority, 24 September 2021.

'Australian Curriculum Version 9.0', Australian Curriculum, Assessment and Reporting Authority, viewed 3 April 2023 , https://v9.australian-curriculum.edu.au.

Ward, Mary, 'Consent Education Unchanged in NSW Schools, Two Years After Public Reckoning', *Sydney Morning Herald*, 28 January 2023.

Yussuf, Ahmed and Walden, Max, 'Multicultural Groups Welcome Federal Government's Move to Collect Ethnicity Data', ABC News, 16 June 2022.

Al Nashar, Nabil, 'Federal Government Criticised for Not Raising Awareness of Multicultural Policies Review', ABC News, 8 March 2023.

'Improving Cultural, Linguistic and Racial Diversity in the APS', Community and Public Service Union, August 2023.

'Speech – National Press Club', Ministers' Media Centre, Ministers of the Education Portfolio, 19 July 2023.

'Multicultural Framework Review', Department of Home Affairs, 16 August 2023.

'Expert Group to Boost Respectful Relationships Education in Schools',
     Ministers' Media Centre, Ministers of the Education Portfolio,
     18 May 2023.

Contributor Biographies

Amanda Hooton

Amanda Hooton is a journalist with the *Sydney Morning Herald* and *The Age* and has been a long-form staff writer with *Good Weekend* for over twenty years. Her work has been recognised with a Walkley Award for Australian journalism and awards at both the Scottish and British British Press Awards. She is the author of *Finding Mr Darcy*.

Arlie Alizzi

Arlie Alizzi is a Yugambeh writer from Queensland currently living on Yawuru Country (Broome). He is an editor for Magabala Books and obtained his PhD in Indigenous Literature in 2021 with a focus on futurism in fiction and film. He is a member of First Nations arts collective this mob, based in Collingwood. As a freelancer, Arlie has written for outlets like the *Sydney Morning Herald*, *Liminal Magazine*, the *Saturday Paper*, ABC, *Memo Review* and *Overland*.

Ceridwen Dovey

Ceridwen Dovey writes both fiction (*Only the Animals; Mothertongues*) and creative non-fiction (*On J.M. Coetzee: Writers on Writers*) and has won an Australian Museum Eureka Award and UNSW Press Bragg Prize for long-form science writing. Her essays have been published by newyorker.com, the *Smithsonian Magazine*, *WIRED*, *VOGUE*, *The Monthly* and *Alexander*. She loves to experiment across genres and is passionate about helping other writers find and hone their voice on the page.

Claire Keenan

Claire Keenan is a journalist and producer. Currently she is working at *Guardian Australia* as a news producer. Previously she was a senior producer and reporter at Junkee media, where she hosted their daily online news and culture show, covering a range of topics including women's health, consent education, politics, social justice and popular culture. When she's not producing, she loves the occasional shift at local Sydney bookstore Ariel Books (where she worked and developed her love for reading during university), and has in the past worked for the Sydney Writers' Festival organising regional programs – a country kid at heart. She got her first writing gig for her local newspaper in Griffith, New South Wales.

Dan Jervis-Bardy

Dan Jervis-Bardy is a federal politics reporter for the *West Australian*, based in Parliament House, Canberra. He was born and raised in Adelaide, and his path to a career in journalism began with a love of sport and passion for writing. He got his start with News Corp Australia, covering council politics and community news across suburban Adelaide. Dan followed his partner to the nation's capital in 2018 and took up a job with the city's daily news-paper, the *Canberra Times*. After stints covering breaking news, urban affairs and ACT politics, he moved into the Canberra press gallery in February 2021.

Esther Linder

Esther Linder is a photojournalist with the Australian Associated Press (AAP) working on Gadigal land (Sydney). Her work has appeared in *The Monthly*, the *Saturday Paper*, *Guardian Australia*, the ABC and elsewhere. She holds a Master of Journalism and a BA in Linguistics, and has previously worked for the United Nations on gender equality practice in the South Caucasus region. Esther's work focuses on the personal ramifications of crises including climate change, gender issues and food security.

Hessom Razavi

Hessom Razavi is an eye surgeon and writer based in Perth. In 1983 his family fled political persecution in Iran to settle in Australia. He has visited the detention centres on Manus Island and Nauru in a medical capacity, writing about these experiences as the Behrouz Boochani Fellow for the *Australian Book Review*. His publication credits include shortlistings for the Newcastle Poetry Prize and *Best Australian Poems 2016*. Hessom is the founder of Lions InReach Vision, an eye health service for refugees, people seeking asylum and Indigenous people in Western Australia.

Liz Gooch

Liz Gooch is a journalist, editor and documentary producer. She has reported from Southeast Asia, Africa and Australia. For the past ten years she has worked as a senior producer for *101 East*,

Al Jazeera's current affairs documentary program, and as a freelance writer. Liz previously worked as a freelance correspondent for the *New York Times* in Malaysia. She has contributed to *Good Weekend Magazine*, CNN, and was a staff reporter for the *South China Morning Post* in Hong Kong and *The Age* in Melbourne. Liz won a Walkley Award with two of her Al Jazeera colleagues for their coverage of the Rohingya refugee crisis.

Maddison Connaughton

Maddison Connaughton is a journalist whose reporting focuses on how global issues affect people on a human scale. Her work has featured in *The Guardian*, the *New York Times*, *Foreign Policy*, *Good Weekend*, the *Japan Times*, *France 24* and more. She was previously editor of the *Saturday Paper*. Before that she was features editor at *Vice*, where she was twice a finalist for the Walkley Award for Young Australian Journalist of the Year for her reporting on teenage refugees of the Syrian War, millennial foreign fighters and criminal justice reform in Australia.

Margaret Simons

Margaret Simons is an award-winning freelance journalist and the author of many books, articles and essays. She is also a journalism academic and Honorary Principal Fellow at the Centre for Advancing Journalism, the University of Melbourne. She has won the Walkley Award for Social Equity Journalism, a Foreign Press Association Award and a number of Quill Awards, including for her reporting from the Philippines with photojournalist Dave Tacon. *Penny Wong: Passion and Principle* is her most recent book.

Matthew Drummond

Matthew Drummond is the editor of the *Australian Financial Review Magazine*, the *Financial Review's* monthly magazine. In 2022 he launched *Fin Magazine*, a quarterly lifestyle title. He has previously been the editor of *AFR Weekend* and worked as the paper's European correspondent. As a journalist he has covered legal affairs as well as banking and finance. In 2008 he was a joint recipient of the Walkley Award for Business Journalism for his investigative pieces on the collapse of stockbroker Opes Prime. Matthew has also worked in marketing at the Sydney Opera House and as a competition lawyer at Mallesons Stephen Jaques.

Michael Brissenden

Michael Brissenden worked as a political journalist and foreign correspondent with the ABC for thirty-five years. He was the political editor for *7.30*, Defence and National Security Correspondent, presenter of the *AM* program, a correspondent in Moscow, Brussels and Washington and for a number of years a reporter with *Four Corners*. He has published both fiction and non-fiction books and is now writing fiction full-time. His first two novels were *The List*, published in 2017, and *Dead Letters*, published in 2021. His next crime novel *Smoke* will be published in Australia by Affirm Press in 2024.

Nick Feik

Nick Feik is the former editor of *The Monthly* magazine. He helmed the publication for eight years, departing in May 2022. During this time, *The Monthly* published eight Walkley Award–winning essays. As a writer Nick has contributed to various Australian and international publications on politics, environmentalism, economics and popular culture. Prior to *The Monthly* he was programmer at the Melbourne International Film Festival.

Paddy Manning

Paddy Manning is a freelance investigative journalist, contributing editor for *The Monthly*, and author of *The Successor: The High-Stakes Life of Lachlan Murdoch* and five other books, including *Body Count: How Climate Change Is Killing Us*, which won the Non-Fiction Prize in the Victorian Premier's Literary Awards 2021. He is completing a PhD on the history of News Corporation.

Penny Craswell

Penny Craswell is a Sydney-based writer, editor and curator, and author of *Reclaimed: New homes from old materials* and *Design Lives Here: Australian interiors, furniture and lighting.* She is a former editor of *Artichoke* magazine, deputy editor of *Indesign* magazine and assistant editor of *Frame* magazine in Amsterdam. She was creative strategy associate at the Australian Design Centre, where she co-directed Sydney Craft Week. She currently writes for *Green* magazine, *Houses* magazine, *Art/Edit* magazine and *NGV Magazine*, and has been published widely in design periodicals, books and online media around the world. She writes a blog called *The Design Writer.*

Sam Elkin

Sam Elkin is a writer, lawyer and co-editor of *Nothing to Hide: Voices of Trans and Gender Diverse Australia* (Allen & Unwin, 2022). Born in England and raised on Noongar land, Sam now lives on unceded Wurundjeri land. Sam's essays have been published in the *Griffith Review, Australian Book Review, Sydney Review of Books* and *Kill Your Darlings*. He hosts the 3RRR radio show *Queer View Mirror* and is a tilde Melbourne Trans & Gender Diverse Film Festival board member. His debut book *Detachable Penis: A Queer Legal Saga* will be released by Upswell Publishing in 2024.

Victoria Laurie

Victoria Laurie is an award-winning feature writer based in Perth. She writes for various publications, including the *Australian Weekend Magazine*, and has worked as a senior reporter for *The Australian* and ABC TV and radio and freelanced for *The Monthly*, *The Bulletin*, *HQ*, *Australian Geographic* and others. She is founder and national co-patron of Women in Media, a not-for-profit initiative to support women working in the sector, and a Walkley Foundation director. She is the author of natural history books *The Kimberley: Australia's Last Great Wilderness*, and *The Southwest: Australia's Biodiversity Hotspot* (UWAP).

Wing Kuang

Wing Kuang is a digital and audio journalist at ABC News, covering national and international affairs. She is also the co-host of SBS podcast *Chinese-ish*, which features young Chinese-Australians exploring their lives and identities. You can see her other work in the *Guardian Australia*, *The Age* and the *Sydney Morning Herald*, Al Jazeera English, the *Saturday Paper*, Hong Kong's *Initium Media* and America's *WhyNot*. Wing graduated from the University of Melbourne with a Master of Journalism in 2020. She's now pursuing a Master of Interpreting and Translation at Western Sydney University. She is proficient in Cantonese and Mandarin.

Discover a
new favourite